RIDER IN THE SKY

How an American Cowboy Built England's First Airplane

John Hulls
with illustrations by David Weitzman

Dedicated to my grandmother Evelyn Hulls, who followed it all with total fascination, from *The Klondyke Nugget,* the Wright brothers' first flight, and Cody's triumphs all the way to Neil Armstrong setting foot on the moon.
She left me knowing the value of a sense of wonder.
—J.H.

Published by Crown Publishers, an imprint of Random House Children's Books, a division of Random House, Inc., New York.
CROWN and colophon are trademarks of Random House, Inc.
www.randomhouse.com/kids

Library of Congress Cataloging-in-Publication Data

Hulls, John.
Rider in the sky : how an American cowboy built England's first airplane / by John Hulls ; with illustrations by David Weitzman.
p. cm.
SUMMARY: Presents the life of the Texas cowboy who, after a varied career that included performing in and running his own Wild West show, became interested in aviation and eventually built and flew England's first airplane in 1908.
Includes bibliographical references and index.

ISBN 0-375-81106-0 (trade) – ISBN 0-375-91106-5 (lib. bdg.)
1. Cody, S. F. (Samuel Franklin), 1861–1913–Juvenile literature. 2. Air pilots–Great Britain–Biography–Juvenile literature. 3. Air pilots–United States–Biography–Juvenile literature. [1. Cody, S. F. (Samuel Franklin), 1861–1913. 2. Air pilots. 3. Aeronautics–History.]
I. Weitzman, David, ill. II. Title.

TL540.C64H85 2003
629.13'092–dc21
[B]
2002041123

Printed in the United States of America
April 2003
10 9 8 7 6 5 4 3 2 1
First Edition

Photo Credits

Courtesy of private sources: pp. 1, 2, 3, 4, 5 (left), 13, 14, 22, 26, 27, 32, 34, 38, 44, 45, 46, 47 (bottom), 48, 49 (both), 51, 55, 56, 57, 60, 61, 62, 65, 68, 69 (right), 70, 72, 73, 76, 80, 83, 84, 85, 86, 88, 89, 90, 91

The photos above were obtained from private sources. There are many scattered collections of Cody images not available to the public, but the Imperial War Museum has recently acquired the Farnborough Museum Archives, which represent the largest collection of Cody images in the UK, including originals or copies of virtually all of the Cody photographs, postcards, and early magazine articles. The archives are currently being cataloged and will soon be made available to the public.

Autry Museum of Western Heritage: p. 5 (right)

Courtesy of the Drachen Foundation: pp. 6, 7, 9, 19 (both), 20 (both), 23, 25, 31, 35, 39 (both), 40 (both), 41, 42, 43 (both), 71

Mary Evans Picture Library: jacket, pp. 79, 81

P. Hare: p. 69 (left)

National Museum of Science and Industry, Science and Society Picture Library: pp. 47 (top), 58, 75, 77, 87

Courtesy of the Wright Brothers Airplane Company: pp. 63, 64

CONTENTS

INTRODUCTION

Kids didn't get to play much in Texas soon after the Civil War; they worked. That was what young Samuel Franklin Cody did, working on cattle drives on the Old Chisholm Trail, up from the Rio Grande in south Texas through Fort Worth, then to Enid, Oklahoma, and Abilene, Kansas, to the railheads from which cattle were sent east. Cody tended the cowboys' horses and helped the cook who worked on the chuck wagon.

The cook was Chinese. In spare moments, when the cattle were grazing and resting for the next leg of the trail, he would craft elegant silk-and-bamboo kites. Thirteen-year-old Cody loved to play with them, watching the painted shapes soar high above the Texas plain. Long after the other cowboys had lost interest, Cody would watch the old man trim and tie the bamboo, then stretch and paint the oiled silk.

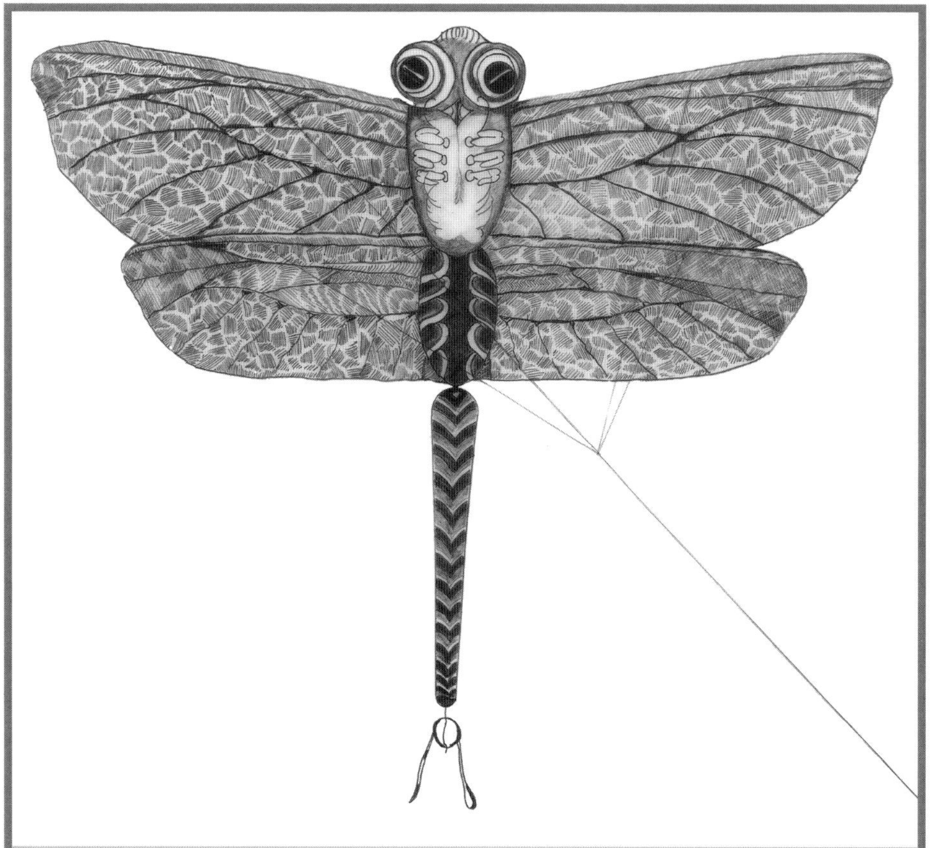

Elegance in bamboo and oiled silk . . . a Chinese kite.

Each time the cook flew a kite, Cody would study every adjustment and detail, learning as he played. "Cook, why do you always paint eyes on the kite before you fly it?"

"Ah, young Cody, if the kite did not have eyes, how would the wind know that the kite was watching?"

Cody was puzzled. "Why is that important?" The old Chinese cook licked his finger and held it up to the wind, measuring its strength and direction from the chill as the moisture evaporated. Then he adjusted the kite lines that formed the bridle, where it attached to the bamboo frame. "Cody, the wind gods are powerful. The kite's eyes must look at them with respect. The kite is asking the wind to lift it high, so it must look at the wind proudly and bravely. If the kite's eyes look down too humbly, so it does not see the wind, it will not be taken up. But a kite looking straight at the wind is too proud; the wind will shake it and throw it to the ground."

Cody picked up the kite and walked downwind as the old cook reeled out the line. Curious, he held the kite's bridle in different positions above his head, watching and feeling the flow of the wind over the kite. If he held the kite straight up and down, with the eyes looking right at the wind so the breeze hit the entire kite at once, it dashed from side to side—he could feel the buffet and shake of the airflow. If he held the bridle so the eyes looked at the ground, there was no lift—the kite was flat, only its top edge exposed to the wind. But in between, right where the old cook had fixed the line to the bridle, the kite lifted steadily, tugging to be released.

"Free the kite," ordered the cook. Standing downwind, Cody held the kite in front of him and thrust it upward into the breeze. As he ran back, the kite soared, hovering almost overhead as he reached the place where the old man held the line.

"Young Cody, I saw what you were doing, making the kite look at the wind in different ways." The cook handed Cody the line.

Cody and the cook stood watching the graceful curve of the kite line tracing an arc toward the kite, hundreds of feet above the grazing longhorns and the cowboys who slowly circled them. The boy thrilled to the kite's upward pull. He had no idea how far the kite's lift would carry him.

ALL THE WORLD'S A STAGE

CHAPTER 1

Born in Texas in the 1860s, Samuel Cody began his youthful career as a cook's helper and apprentice cowhand—but this was just the start of his adventures. By the time he was a young man, Cody was already a skilled marksman, lasso artist, and broncobuster, able to tame even the wildest mustang. But the truth of Cody's early life is lost in a mixture of fact, flimflam, and showmanship. He claimed to have been born in 1861, but after his death, records would surface showing the real date as 1867.

As Cody's family tells the story, in his early twenties Cody met an Englishman named Blackburne Davis who was fascinated with American horses. Davis arranged for Cody to bring some mustangs back to England for him and train them: another adventure, a new country. Cody leaped at the chance.

He didn't count on Davis's daughter, Lela, herself a skilled horsewoman who shared her father's interest in the wild American mustangs. It was love at first sight. After only one more trip delivering horses from Texas to England, Cody returned to America with Lela as his bride.

They settled on a cattle ranch, where Cody

quickly became top hand. Soon two sons, Vivian and Leon, were added to the Cody family. But the Texas cattle industry took a turn for the worse. Cody was forced to send his young family back to England while he sought another way to earn a living.

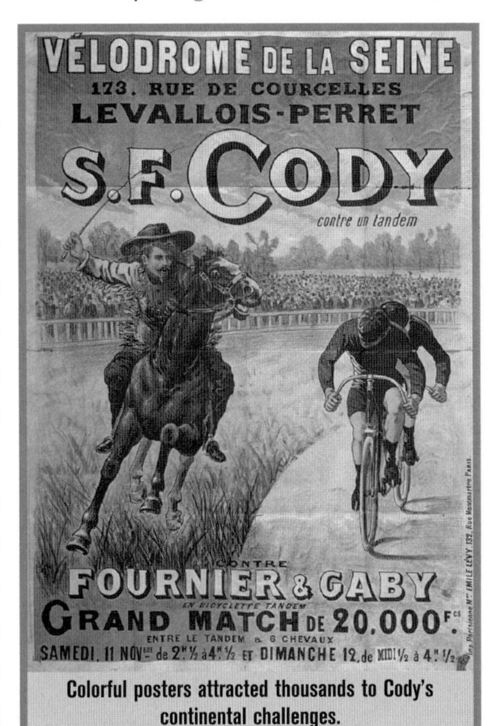

Colorful posters attracted thousands to Cody's continental challenges.

Cody turned this misfortune into an adventure. He rode cross-country to Seattle and boarded a steamboat to Skagway and the Alaskan gold fields, to seek his fortune in the frozen north. He survived the rugged winters and was fascinated by the landscape's grandeur, but he never struck it rich. Since he had promised Lela he would be gone only two years, he left Alaska and worked his way toward the east. He tried his hand at cattle drives again, working up from Texas to the northern states. But the worst blizzards in American history struck in 1886, and in Montana 90 percent of the cattle either froze or starved in what the ranchers called "the Big Die-Up." The cattle industry collapsed. Cody was left trying to make ends meet by broncobusting and training horses in San Antonio.

It was there that fortune again touched Cody's life. Adam Forepaugh was a well-known Wild West show promoter. He had made a fortune bringing what he claimed was a show of the "Old West" to the crowded cities of the East Coast. The sharpshooting cowboys with their lasso tricks, the elaborately dressed Indian chiefs, and even buffalo herds traveled from city to city. The buckskin-fringe jackets, wide white hats, and nickel-plated six-shooters had far more to do with the image presented by the popular five-cent cowboy novels than they had to do with the reality of the Old West. But the East Coast crowds couldn't get enough of these tales of the frontier. Forepaugh had once brought "Buffalo Bill's Wild West Show" to New York; starring William F. Cody (no relation to Samuel), it was the biggest and most successful of the frontier shows. The public liked his mythical image of the Wild West hero.

Now Forepaugh needed another hit—but he had just lost his top marksman. Forepaugh had heard other cowboys telling tales of Samuel Cody's superb horsemanship and uncanny marksmanship. Desperate for a new "lead cowboy," Forepaugh sought him out. Cody was hired on the spot, provided he adopt the fringed buckskin and long hair of the popular frontier-cowboy image. Samuel Cody was a natural showman—he enjoyed the skill and theatrics of presenting himself as a hero of the Old West and enthusiastically adopted many of the same mannerisms as Buffalo Bill as he toured from city to city.

The audiences loved Cody's exuberant performances and marveled at his shooting, riding, and roping. Forepaugh took advantage of Samuel Cody's similarity in both name and appearance to Buffalo Bill (William F. Cody) and took his show all over the East Coast, billing him as "Captain Cody, King of the Cowboys."

Although Cody was now earning enough to support his family, they could not travel from show to show. He missed them tremendously. Then Lela and her father had an idea. Why not start a Wild West show in England? Cody's role model, Buffalo Bill, had enjoyed great success in Europe. Might not Cody do the same, on a more modest scale? Cody could not turn down a new challenge, especially one that would reunite him with his family. Thanking Forepaugh for all his teaching, Cody boarded a steamer for London.

Cody had showmanship in his blood. On his arrival he embraced every opportunity for publicity. At that time, Europe was at the height of the bicycling craze. The modern bike with pneumatic tires had made cheap transportation available at reasonable cost. Almost overnight, it seemed, everybody had one, and soon bicycle racing became a major sport. Cody arranged challenges between himself, on horseback, and the leading bicycle racers of the day. His first race was with Meyer, the French national champion.

The contest was set at the Levallois Trotting Club, near Paris. Cody would ride ten horses in relay; Meyer could have as many bikes as he wanted. They would race around the track four hours a day, for three days—a grueling test of man, horse, and machine. The public was convinced that the French champion and the bicycle would defeat the upstart American and his horses.

The race was a thrilling duel. The lead switched back and forth as horse and bike raced neck and neck. Cody's showmanship days had left him a little out of shape for so arduous a contest, but he pushed himself hard, often leaping off

Cody just barely beats the French champion to the finish line.

one horse directly onto the back of the next fresh mount. Taking the lead at the very end of the race, Cody forged across the finish line in first place. He had barely enough energy to shake Meyer's hand when the cyclist rode up and offered his congratulations. The crowd went wild at the surprise victory,

The Cody family of legend. Counterclockwise: Cody, Lela, Vivian, Edward, and Leon. Decades later, it would be revealed that the boys were actually Lela's children from a previous marriage. Edward was always billed as a "relative," but Vivian and Leon were presented as Cody's own children, and would claim for the rest of their lives that Cody was their father.

and Cody's European career was launched.

Cody held races and shooting exhibitions in all the capitals of Europe. He swore to Lela that the family would never be separated again. He set about making this possible in his usual imaginative but straightforward manner: he gave the entire family roles in his performances.

Cody taught the boys to shoot and ride; Lela, already a skilled rider, became an expert markswoman. The family toured Europe for two seasons. The public loved their flashy shooting tricks. Cody shot apples off the boys' heads while standing backward looking in a mirror, and Leon and Vivian hit impossibly small targets while dangling upside down from their father's arms. Lela stood in a frame that had her outline cut in it, surrounded by twenty glass balls. Cody smashed them all with twenty shots in twenty seconds. (Lela would wear red tights for this act, so if one of the low-powered bullets grazed her, the blood would not show.) At outdoor performances, Cody and the boys performed sharpshooting feats from horseback, Cody breaking glass spheres thrown into the air as he rode by at full gallop.

As much as Cody admired these Buffalo Bill–style Wild West displays, he felt something was lacking. Also, after the birth of his son Frank in Switzerland in 1895, he wanted to stop traveling all over Europe and return to England. Putting on an exhibition at the Alexandria Palace in London, he realized that a Wild West show was a series of stunts—but it needed a story to hold it together. The newspapers of the day were carrying tales of the Klondike gold finds in Dawson, Alaska. Cody's fertile imagination linked his Wild West experiences with his recollections of Alaska, and *The Klondyke Nugget* was born. Though Cody's only schooling was what his mother had taught him, he penned a play in which gold prospectors, Indians, sheriffs, saloon girls, and bad men engaged in all the ambition, greed, jealousy, and raw passion that true love, gunplay, lynchings, and gold nuggets could evoke.

This lurid, bloodcurdling melodrama supposedly showed the realities of frontier life. Actually, it was more a showcase for the Cody family's theatrical talents and Wild West skills. Cody designed elaborate sets, including a gold mine shown in cross section, with miners laboring in the tunnels, a working mine hoist in the "snow-capped mountain" above, a courtroom with a window big enough for a horse to jump through, and a bridge over a chasm, with a cabin perched precariously on the edge.

5

Scenes from *The Klondyke Nugget* shown in one of Cody's colorful posters.

Lela, of course, was the heroine. But Cody was not the hero. That role fell to his son Leon. Cody played the villainous sheriff, who kills a gold miner to get his giant gold nugget, then tries to frame Leon and have him lynched by the saloon crowd. Leon is saved by a faithful Indian companion, who jumps his horse through the courtroom window and rides off with Leon.

But the evil sheriff does not give up; he ambushes Leon and throws him down the chasm. Telling Lela that Leon is dead, the sheriff begs her to run away with him. She loyally refuses, so he ties her to a barrel of gunpowder and lights the fuse. Leon's trusty Indian companion attacks the evil sheriff, and they fight to the death with bowie knives. At the last second, Leon climbs out of the chasm and frees Lela. Mounting Leon's horse, they leap the chasm as the gunpowder explodes and the bridge collapses.

This last scene was invariably greeted with thunderous applause. The play was a huge success.

The lurid climax of *The Klondyke Nugget* displayed in another of Cody's posters.

BIGGER KITES

CHAPTER 2

"Hey, Dad, the new exploding bridge worked well last night."

But Samuel Cody was not listening to his son Leon. Something else was on his mind as the family sat around the table for a leisurely Sunday breakfast one morning. Lela was trying for the umpteenth time to make Texas-cowboy flapjacks with English ingredients.

Sunday theatrical performances were prohibited in much of England, so the Codys relaxed that day from their strenuous *Klondyke Nugget* regime. Instead of answering his son, Cody set down his newspaper. "I've always wanted to build a really big kite. Now I can!"

Cody had been reading about kite experiments. An Australian researcher, Lawrence Hargrave, had come to England in 1899 to seek funding for his experiments with kites. A serious scientist, Hargrave had been working on cellular, or box-shaped, kites since 1893. His design consisted of a rectangular, boxlike frame with fabric stretched in a band around either end. It was far more stable than all previous kite designs, and the braced box structure made it very strong and light. The "Hargrave Box Kite" was even available in toy stores. Its structural effectiveness was the basis of many early flying-machine experiments. Hargrave's kites were already used in meteorological research, much as Benjamin Franklin had used kites for his experiments on electricity over a hundred years earlier. The military was becoming interested in aerial observation, too, and kites seemed to provide a perfect opportunity for these tactics.

A publicity picture of Cody and young Frank.

The newspaper article that Cody was reading told of the experiments of Army major B.F.S. Baden-Powell. His brother, also an Army major, was one of the heroes of the Boer War in South Africa, where the Army had used tethered balloons for artillery spotting for the first time. When spotters high above the battlefield told the gunners where their shells had landed, the gunners could adjust their artillery weapons with devastating accuracy. Baden-Powell's brother's experience had revealed that balloons, though often very effective, could not be used in high winds. He and his brother had hoped to come up with a stable man-lifting kite, but they had yet to find a solution. Baden-Powell had succeeded in lifting a man a modest height from the ground with a group of kites tied together, before abandoning this approach as dangerously unstable.

At the time of these experiments, there were several approaches to flying. Lighter-than-air balloons had been used by armies as early as the American Civil War, using hot air or gas to lift an observer. These balloons were either moored to the ground by a cable or floated freely, relying on the wind to carry them where they wanted to go. Researchers like Baden-Powell were experimenting with kites, a heavier-than-air device in which the force of the wind provides the lift. Kites are in many ways a wing tethered to the ground and held at the correct angle to the wind to provide lift. People were also experimenting with free-flight using gliders or powered aircraft. Experimenters such as Otto Lilienthal believed that by learning to fly gliders, they could learn the secrets of control and then progress to powered flight. Others, like Hiram Maxim, the inventor of the machine gun, spent a fortune on experiments on powered aircraft, believing that they would just soar stably through the air.

The balloon people were starting to have some success with powered balloons held to a rigid frame that carried an engine and propellers, but little progress was being made on heavier-than-air flight. Lilienthal was fatally injured in a crash in 1896, and interest in all heavier-than-air experiments almost vanished, except for a few kite enthusiasts such as Hargrave and Baden-Powell. It would be up to the Wright brothers to lead the march down the road from kites to gliders to powered flight.

Cody felt that kites were the way to fly, although he could see the problems of stability and control. However, as Cody told the boys, the old Chinese cook's kites had been very steady, even in the high winds of the Texas plains. Remembering the upward tug of the kite, Cody could not see any real reason why it was impossible to make a kite big enough and steady enough to lift a person. The idea latched firmly on to Cody's imagination. The family was off on the start of a new adventure.

Once breakfast was finished, the family trooped to Windsor Great Park, the preferred venue for kite flying by the leading experimenters of the day. The Codys watched as members of the Imperial War College and Royal Meteorological Society flew their kites.

Several people recognized Cody from *The Klondyke Nugget* and were surprised at his interest in kite attachments and angles and how well the kites lifted. And Cody was delighted to meet the very same Major B.F.S. Baden-Powell he had just read about in his newspaper.

The men took an instant liking to each other, as Baden-Powell regaled Cody with tales of his experiments. He related how he had finally succeeded in lifting a man a hundred feet in the air, with stabilizing ropes held on either side to stop the kite from dashing to the ground. It was impossible to get very high that way, and they abandoned the dangerous tests with the side ropes, as it was considered bad form to kill your fellow collaborators. However, the experiments did prove that the force of the wind could indeed lift a man, even if there were many problems that would have to be solved before it became a practical method of flight.

The men spent the whole afternoon in discussion as they watched the various experimenters test their kites. Cody intrigued Baden-Powell with stories of the old Chinese cook and his delicate silken kites, and he listened to the Army major's accounts of the different kiting methods he had tried, from square kites to round kites to many kites tied together, all in an attempt to get sufficient lifting power and stability. They both agreed that it was a fascinating problem, and Baden-Powell told Cody he was more than welcome to join in the kiting experiments.

That evening, Cody and the boys covered the dinner table with kite sketches. They settled finally on a large box kite, along Hargrave lines. Cloth would be the kite skin; finding cloth was no problem, since it was used on all their stage sets, but Cody was uncertain about frame material. He settled on bamboo and located a shop in London, F. Westbury and Sons, that supplied him with the strong, light woody reed.

Off to the theater workshops the family went. Cody showed the boys how to cut and lash together a bamboo frame. He sketched patterns for the canvas with elaborate sleeves and pockets, so the kite could be quickly assembled at the field. Lela stitched up the canvas shapes.

What emerged was a massive box kite, more than four times Cody's height. A couple of Sundays later, the family loaded up the kite, rolls of strong piano wire, and a large picnic lunch and headed off in a horse and buggy to Windsor Great Park.

One of the first people to greet them was Major Baden-Powell, who looked askance as Leon, Viv, and young Frank—the three Cody boys—assembled the huge kite. Cody, carrying a large metal stake and a sledgehammer, walked to the upwind side of the park.

Cody drove his stake deep into the ground. Leon ran up, unrolling a drum of piano wire, which Cody attached to the stake and tied down so that it couldn't unwind.

Leaving Leon to tend the anchored end of the cable, Cody and Baden-Powell walked back to where the giant box kite lay on the ground. As the cook had done many years before, Cody licked his finger and held it up, gauging the strength and direction of the breeze. Baden-Powell tore off some leaves of grass and threw them into the air. There was a good, steady breeze, not too strong. As Cody adjusted the angle of the kite and fastened the piano-wire line to the bridle, he told Baden-Powell the cook's tale of how the wind gods look at kites. Baden-Powell could see that Cody had a real feel for the lift of the kite.

Cody held the cable about thirty feet in front of the huge kite as Baden-Powell and Vivian lifted the front. The breeze flowed under it, and it rose a few feet off the ground. Cody hung on to the cable, stopping it from climbing any higher.

But Cody was not satisfied with the kite's adjustment. He moved along the line toward the kite, pulling the wire down as he went. The major and Vivian grabbed the bottom of the kite as it settled. Cody adjusted the bridle to make the kite flatter to the wind and returned to his position holding on to the wire. This time, when the wind got under the kite, Cody could barely hold it down. Testing the upward pull of the line, he was pleased.

Cody released the line and the kite swept upward over a hundred feet, pulling the wire taut with a satisfying twang. The whole group of kite fliers walked to where Leon was watching the drum that held the piano wire. Baden-Powell offered his congratulations on the successful first flight of such a monster kite, but Cody clearly felt that the kite could get much more lift from the breeze. He studied the kite as it floated lazily overhead, swaying gently with the shifts in the wind. Occasionally Cody pulled on the line to test the force of the lift, a look of studied concentration on his face.

Cody never thought small, as shown by his giant box kite.

Lela joined them with the picnic hamper, and they sat on the grass eating lunch, watching the huge kite float above them, dancing from side to side with each little change in the breeze.

By now the other kite fliers were watching Cody's monster with interest and anticipation. All afternoon Cody and the boys experimented with different bridle angles. Each time they adjusted the angle of the bridle to make the kite flatter to the wind, the kite flew higher but became more unstable, darting from side to side before finally lifting straight upward. Cody was testing his kite's limits. He was about to find them.

They went through the now familiar routine of hauling the kite down and adjusting the bridle. Baden-Powell was helping them with intensifying interest.

Cody clearly felt that he was close to the maximum lifting angle of the kite, the point at which, as the old cook once put it, the kite was getting too bold. The lift of the kite was strong enough that Cody had great difficulty in holding the line down while they tested the angle. He knew if the kite pulled the line out of his hands, there was no way of knowing what it might do as it dashed from side to side. Cody cautioned his helpers to stay clear of the kite when they let it go.

As the major and the boys sprinted upwind, the kite leaped into the air, yanking the cable from Cody's hands. Every piece of cloth and bamboo strummed and vibrated with the wind's force. It zoomed straight up, arched over spectacularly, and dove vertically into the ground with a splintering crash. The destruction was absolute. Everyone looked at Cody, studying his reaction. He stood, hands on hips, contemplating the debris.

Baden-Powell saw the fire in Cody's eyes. The speculation that had stayed in Cody's mind since his kite-flying days in Texas was answered. He could make a kite that could lift a man . . . but how to control it? Baden-Powell, pulled by the same vision of flight, knew the American would return with a new kite—and soon. No doubt about it.

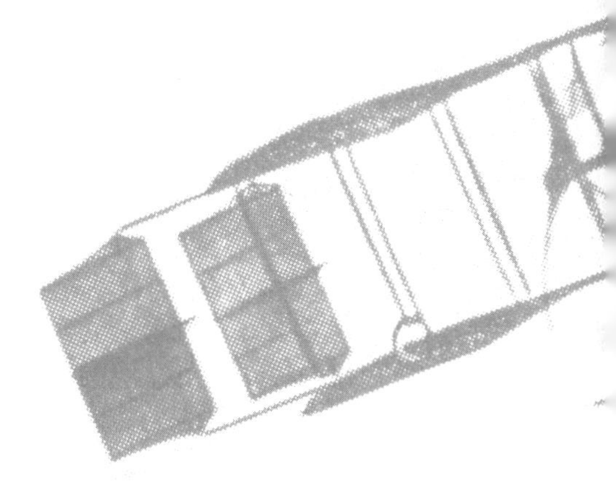

~ Meanwhile . . . Kites, Krakatoa, and Cold, Cold Weather ~

Did Cody leave Texas because of a volcano? Twice in the nineteenth century volcanoes significantly altered the climate of the world—not to mention people's lives. When Tambora, near Bali, erupted in April 1815 with the force of a billion tons of TNT, it killed all the vegetation on the islands of Bali and Lombok. Eight thousand people were engulfed by the lava and volcanic ash. Hundreds of thousands more all over Asia died from the resulting famine. News of the event, carried by sailing ships, took seven months to reach Europe and America. It was old news and received scant attention, only a brief article in the London *Times*. No one made the connection between the volcano and the disastrous winter that followed. William Turner, whose earlier paintings are prized for their "imaginative" sunsets, was not imagining at all. He was accurately recording sunsets turned purple and red by the dust of Tambora.

Then, in 1883, a nearby volcano, Krakatoa, erupted with a much smaller force, yet still sent huge clouds of dust into the atmosphere that rapidly encircled the globe.

This time the telegraph brought news of the massive eruption to the world within hours. Stories in magazines and newspapers sparked widespread interest in meteorology and the effects of volcanoes on the weather. When the Royal Society met in 1888, it was to consider the effects of Krakatoa on world climates. As it began collecting data on the eruption, it became clear that an event in faraway Asia could affect the lives of people in America and Europe. French scientists measured a 20 percent drop in the intensity of the sun. From America came reports that a severe winter had wiped out the Texas cattle industry, putting Cody and thousands of other cowboys and ranchers out of work.

The next year, 1889, dubbed by the press as "the year without summer," it rained or snowed every day in England. The Thames River froze over. And New England suffered the coldest weather in two hundred years.

So it was that a volcanic eruption in the South Pacific put cowhand Cody out of work in Texas and created a purpose for his high-altitude kites. Scientists, anxious to chart and measure the upper winds, would soon ask Cody if his kites could carry their instruments. Cody did so, spectacularly, in 1902, his kites lifting the instruments many thousands of feet higher than they had ever reached before—nearly three miles into the upper atmosphere.

UNDERSTANDING THE WIND

CHAPTER 3

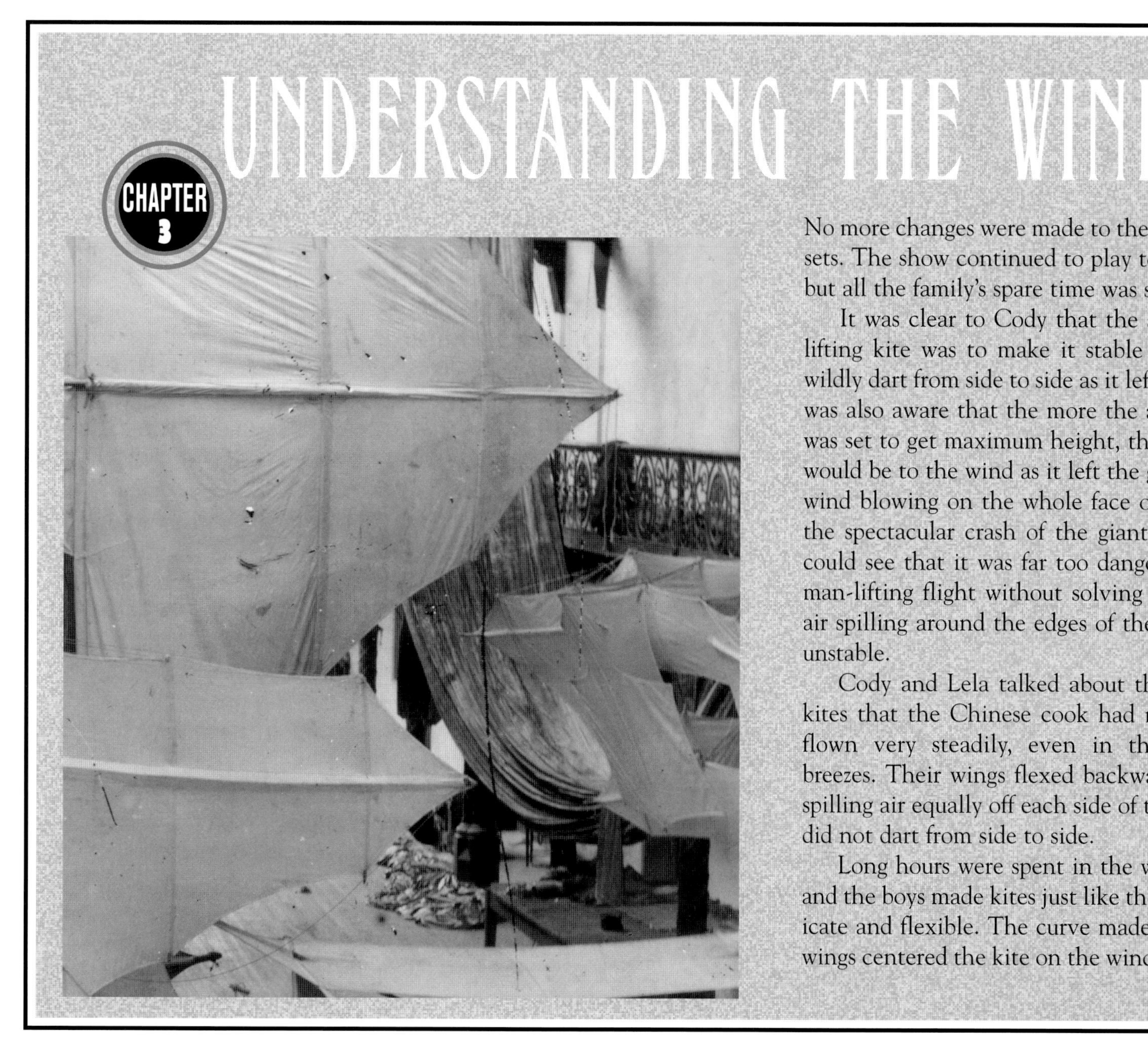

No more changes were made to the *Klondyke Nugget* sets. The show continued to play to packed houses, but all the family's spare time was spent on kites.

It was clear to Cody that the secret to a man-lifting kite was to make it stable so it would not wildly dart from side to side as it left the ground. He was also aware that the more the angle of the kite was set to get maximum height, the flatter the kite would be to the wind as it left the ground, with the wind blowing on the whole face of the kite. From the spectacular crash of the giant box kite, Cody could see that it was far too dangerous to attempt man-lifting flight without solving the problems of air spilling around the edges of the kite, making it unstable.

Cody and Lela talked about the light, flexible kites that the Chinese cook had made. They had flown very steadily, even in the strong Texas breezes. Their wings flexed backward in the wind, spilling air equally off each side of the kites, so they did not dart from side to side.

Long hours were spent in the workshops. Cody and the boys made kites just like the old cook's, delicate and flexible. The curve made by the bending wings centered the kite on the wind. But how could

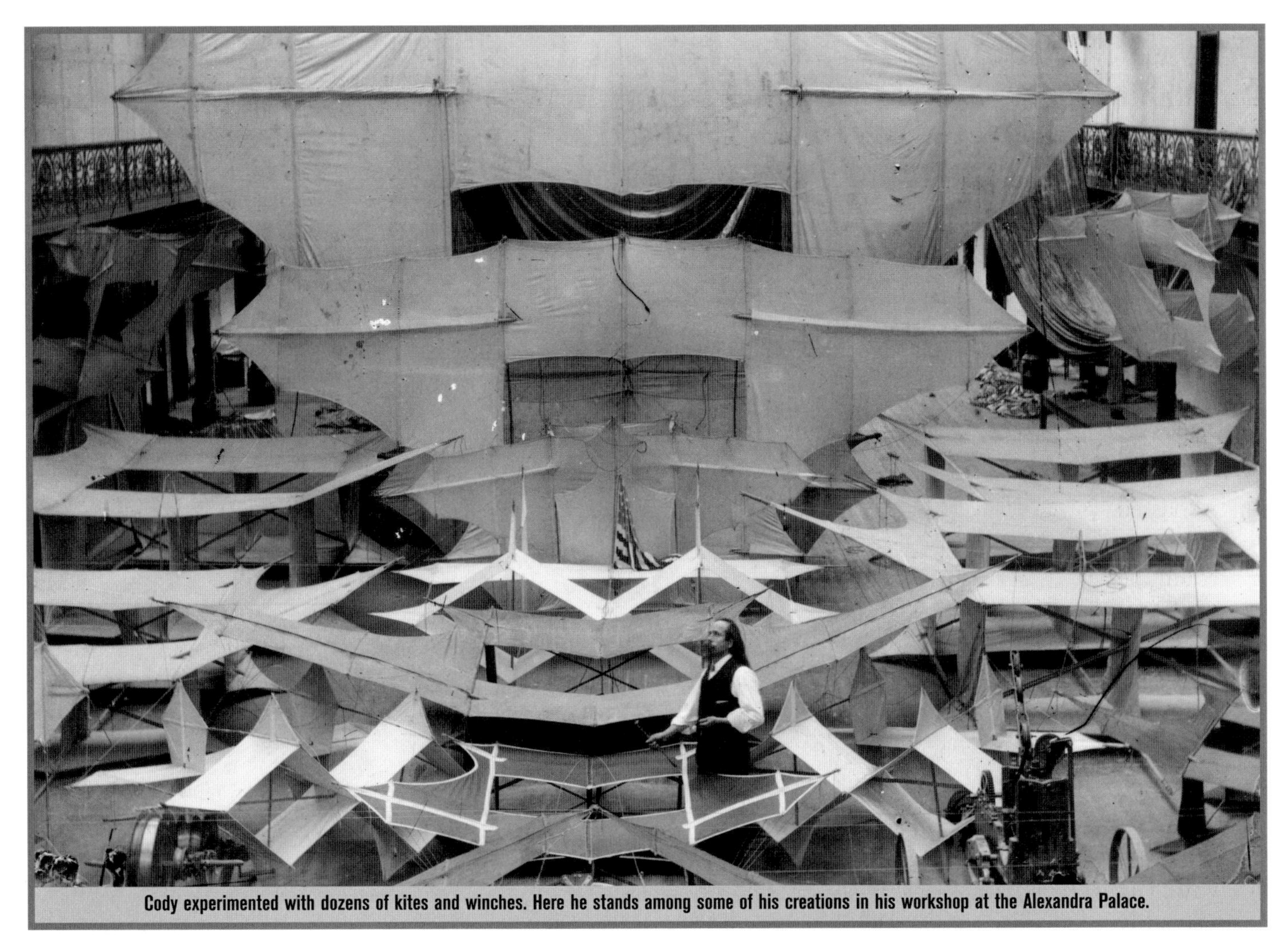

Cody experimented with dozens of kites and winches. Here he stands among some of his creations in his workshop at the Alexandra Palace.

they make a stable, strong structure big enough to lift a person? They had to find out.

Many ideas emerged from the workshops. When there was not enough wind to test them, the boys would dash madly up and down the street pulling the kites while their father watched. It was clear that the angle of the wings was very important. Their designs evolved from the flexible wings of the Chinese kites to ones with rigid wings set at an angle, but Cody was still looking for the combination of strength, stability, and lifting power that would get him airborne. Finally, he hit on a design that showed special promise. It had the body of a box kite—diagonal struts that held the body shape extended outward and supported big, batlike wings at the front, smaller ones at the back. It looked sleek and purposeful.

Cody, Lela, and the boys set to work. Soon an 18-foot-wide monster kite emerged from the workshops. It also boasted a winch with spare cable drums, so line could be added as the kite climbed. Cody's Windsor acquaintances were impressed with both the kite and the winch system. They were further amazed when the kite, after darting once or twice in the turbulent air near the ground, climbed steadily skyward as Cody unwound reel after reel of cable. Soon the kite was a small dot high in the sky, rock-steady in the stiff breeze.

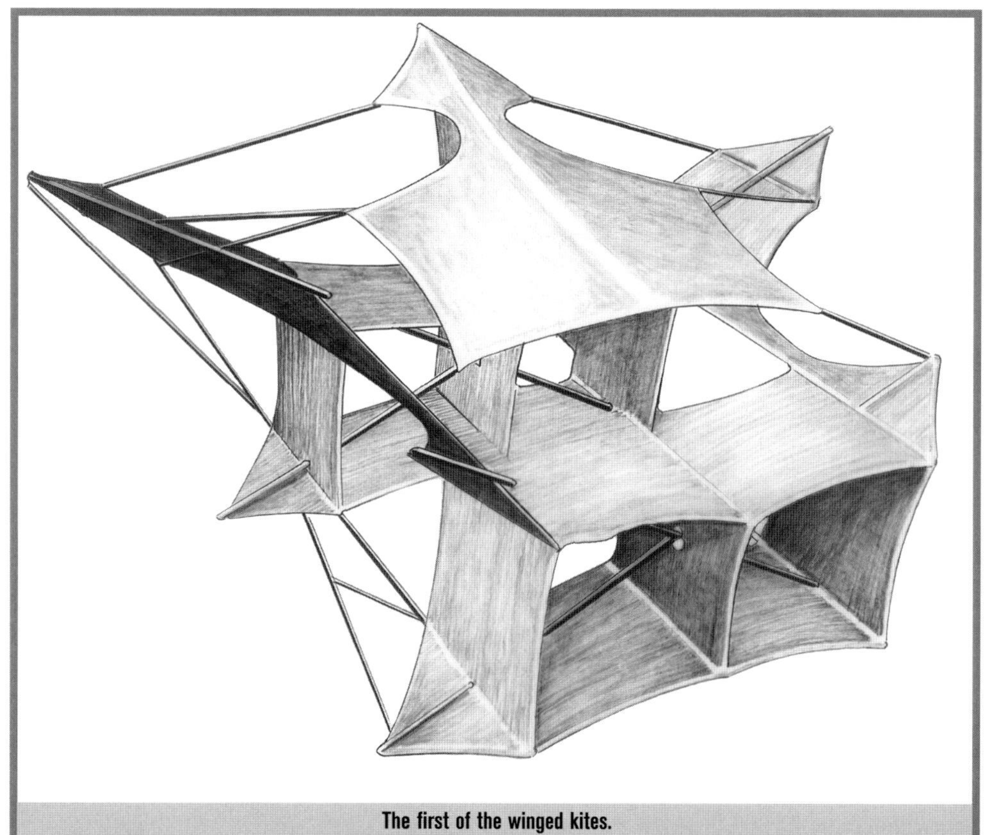

The first of the winged kites.

Baden-Powell was the first to offer congratulations. Cody was pleased, yet something still troubled him. He could well imagine that even though the kite was incredibly stable once it had risen high enough, the rough air near the ground could still hurl the kite to earth. A kite big enough to lift a man plus any length of cable would be a real monster, far too powerful to control near the ground. Cody had quickly run headlong into the problem that had stopped all the other kite scientists and experimenters, but he was not about to give up.

Baden-Powell had taken many photographs of his own experiments. They showed four linked kites and a spider's web of cables to hold the kites directly on the wind. He had hoped that by preventing the kites from swinging around freely, they would be more stable. It hadn't worked very well, and Baden-Powell told Cody that they had abandoned this line of experimentation. It showed no more stability or lifting power than one big kite.

Baden-Powell's string of kites planted an idea in Cody's mind, though. Why not use a *chain* of kites to lift the cable high into steady air? Because the "lifting kites" up in the steady breeze would give the line stability, he could then "fly" the giant man-lifting kite up and down the cable, without its being dashed sideways into the ground. He could also attach lines to the giant kite to control the angle of the kite in flight, thus producing only as much lift as he wanted! Cody was soon lost in the design details.

The next field trip, in the spring of 1901, looked like a parade, as the Cody family, now assisted by stagehands from *The Klondyke Nugget,* carried out all the new lifting kites, the big new winch, and the large man-lifting kite, along with the trolley and control cables. For the first time, a seat hung below the biggest of the kites. It took a while to get everything put together. The breeze was steady as the boys assembled the lifting kites while Cody rigged the winch and anchored it. Cody hooked the "topknot" kite, an especially stable kite with an extra lifting surface on the front, to the main line and launched it. As the line unreeled, they sent more cable-lifting kites up the line. Part of Cody's design was an ingenious clamping system that enabled each lifting kite to fly up the line to a predetermined spot, where it would clamp onto the cable and take its share of the weight of the line. As each lifting kite slid up the line, even more cable could be unreeled as the topknot kite rose steadily higher and higher, far above the rough air near the ground.

Cody and the boys rapidly assembled the man-lifting kite

Cody at the winch

and the trolley that held it to the line. To try out the system, he had arranged "up" and "down" control cables so he could fly the man-lifting kite from the ground for the first tests. While Cody was very brave, he was not foolhardy, so he set about testing to see how the whole system behaved before he attempted to fly himself. He had brought along a large log, about his weight, which the boys tied to the sling chair suspended from the pulley. Assisted by half a dozen stagehands, they hooked the giant man-lifting kite to the cable, now hanging from a chain of lifting kites flying steadily overhead.

Cody tugged the "up" control cable, which set the kite in the lifting position. To the boys' cheers, the huge kite gently lifted the test log from the ground and glided smoothly up the main cable until it floated steadily 100 feet above them. Cody still looked concerned. Slowly he pulled on the line controlling the descent, and the man-lifting kite and the log slid gently back to earth. Cody repeated the cycle several times, his face finally breaking into a grin. It was stable. It was controllable. It was really working!

Cody was ready to fly.

The log used for the test weight was removed from the sling seat, and Cody climbed aboard. The boys raised the wings of the man-lifting kite. The wind picked the kite up and it

The man-lifting kite flying up the cable

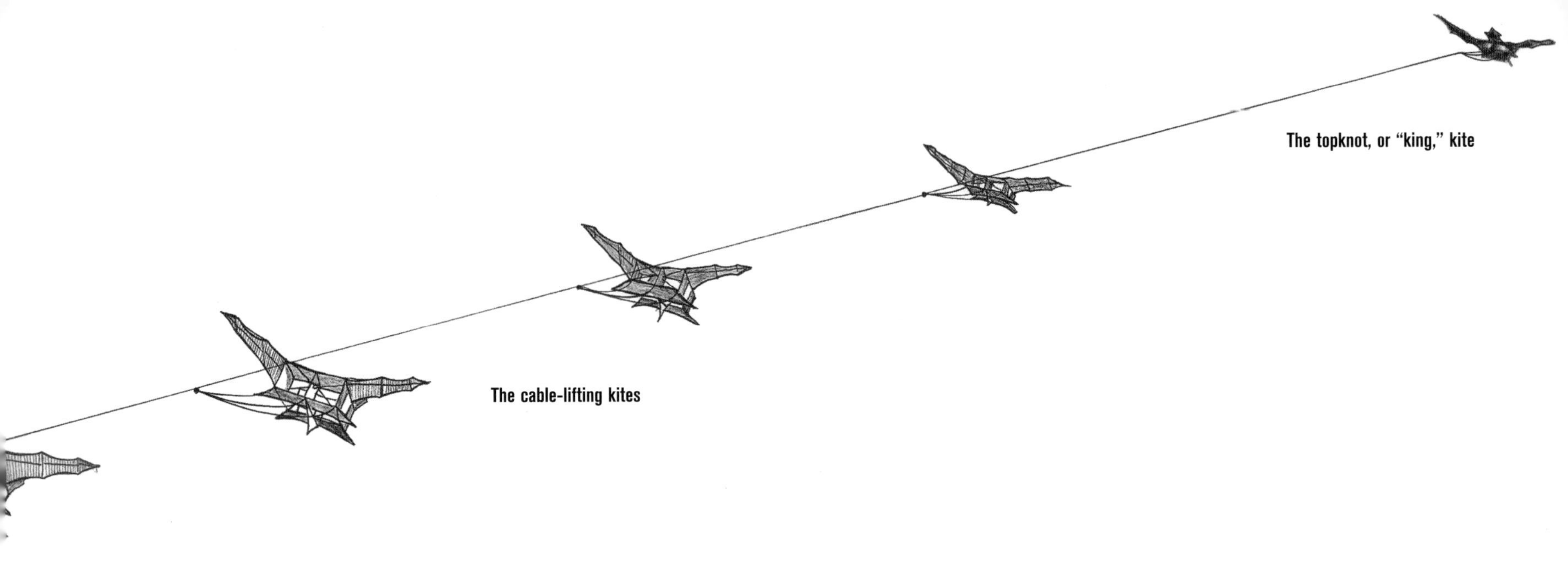

danced on the line, just above Cody's head, as he adjusted the control lines. The kite tugged harder as Cody increased the angle. Ever so gently, the kite and the trolley glided up the cable, lifting Cody from the ground. He added a little more angle and the kite slid 100 feet up the line, carrying Cody with it. He paused for a minute, then gently tugged on the "down" control cable. The kite tilted down a few degrees. As Cody glided gently back to earth, the small crowd of onlookers burst into wild cheering.

But Cody was not done for the day. He talked things over with Lela and the boys. They were all well pleased with the stability, and Cody was delighted with the effectiveness of his control system. Nobody had seen anything that would cause concern, and the breeze was steady. The lifting kites floated gently, high above them.

Cody climbed into the seat again and took the control cables in his hands. This time the kite did not stop at 100 feet but kept climbing toward the lifting kites over 1,000 feet above. Cody stopped and finally took a moment to relax and look at the amazed onlookers and the world beneath him, spread out like a map. He was really flying!

Cody was the first person in history to create a controllable man-lifting kite, a heavier-than-air machine. Nearly all the other experimenters in manned flight were using balloons, lifting with either hot air or hydrogen, either tethered to the ground or blown along at the mercy of the air currents. Europe had abandoned soaring flight after the death of German scientist Otto Lilienthal in 1896.

But in the United States, the Wright brothers were making progress with glider experiments on the windy sand dunes of

Kitty Hawk, North Carolina. However, they were running into control problems and could not get the lift from the wings that they planned. They persevered with their experiments and would soon pioneer their own design of wind tunnel to discover the secrets of lift. For the Wrights, flight had gone from being a sport to being a serious scientific study. As Cody worked to perfect his kites, the Wrights struggled with the control of their glider. It would take another year, until 1902, before they finally got it right.

On the other side of the Atlantic, Cody and the family did not rest on their accomplishment. Cody's imagination and ingenuity had found a way to master flight from the power of the wind. He had overcome the control and stability problems that had frustrated some of the best scientific minds of the time. He had already flown higher than anyone else in a heavier-than-air machine. Only balloons had carried anyone higher. By October 1901, Cody felt that he had developed his kite system to the point that he should protect his invention. He filed British Patent Application 23,566, entitled "Improvements in Kites and Apparatus for Same." And he wrote to the War Office, offering his kites to the military for artillery observation.

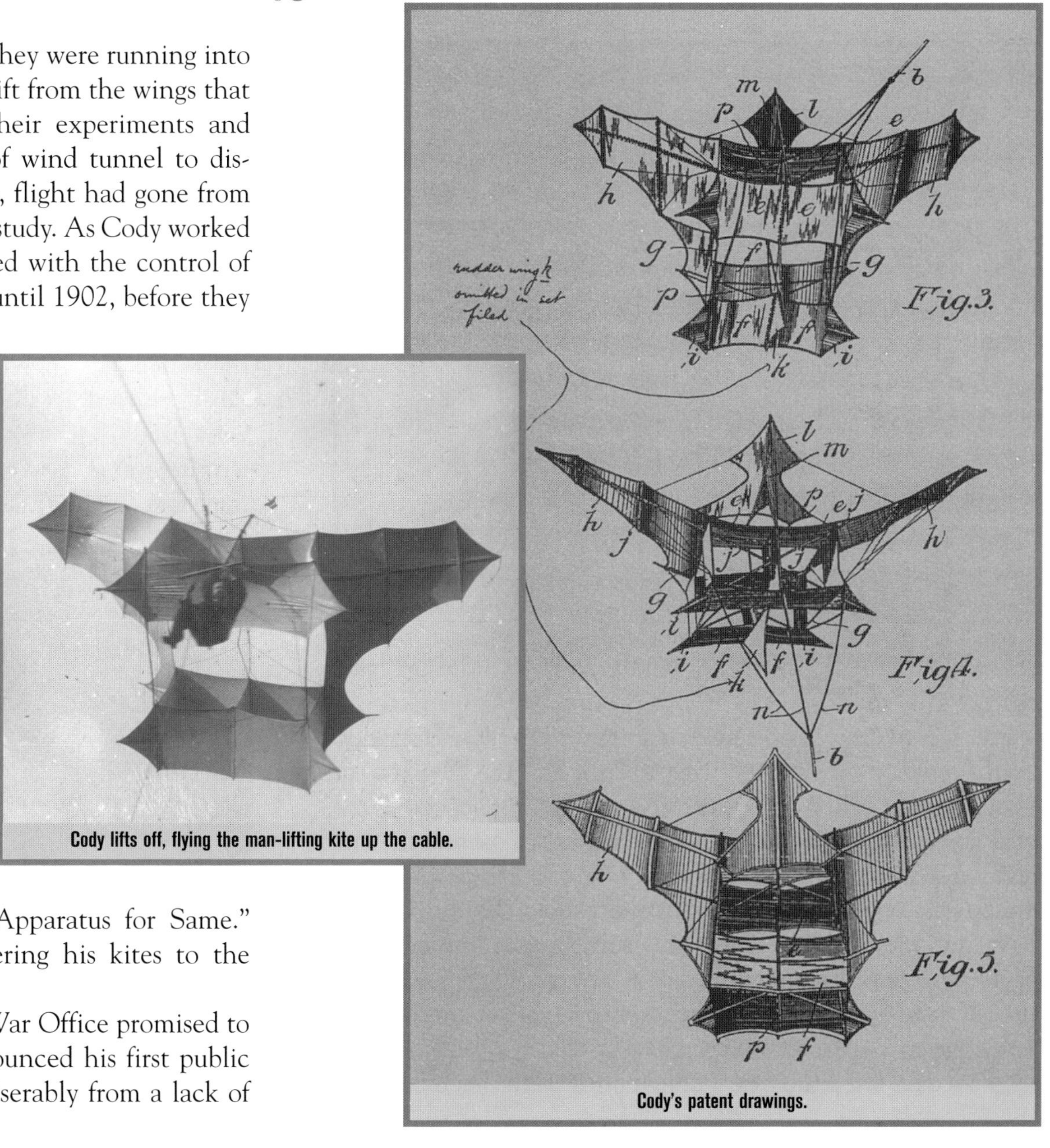

Cody lifts off, flying the man-lifting kite up the cable.

Cody's patent drawings.

A brief telegram response from the War Office promised to send an observer. Impatient, Cody announced his first public demonstration at Wanstead. It failed miserably from a lack of

THE COWBOY MEETS THE COLONELS

CHAPTER 4

Major Trollope visited Cody again in mid-January 1902. This time Cody flew the carrier kite himself. Trollope was so impressed by Cody's trip aloft that he told Cody he would introduce him to Colonel J.L.B. Templer, the Army's staunchest proponent of flight.

A great bear of a man, Templer had started the Army's balloon program by sheer drive and force of personality. He had become a hero when his artillery-spotting balloons brought key victories in the Boer War. Templer was famous in Army circles for his impressive waxed mustache. He claimed that "one did not really have a proper mustache unless it could be seen from behind!" Cody and Templer hit it off immediately, and Cody was so taken with this style of mustache that he adopted it himself.

With the enthusiastic response from Trollope and Templer, Cody believed the military would soon accept the usefulness of his invention. But the performance of his kites was matched by the inertia of the War Office. Months dragged by without progress.

Never one to sit still, Cody, along with his boys, continued to develop the kites and the winch system. Leon built his own kites for the many contests held both by the Aeronautical and the

Meteorological Societies, competing to see who could fly highest. The contest entry lists nearly always showed Samuel and Leon Cody, Major Baden-Powell, C. S. Rolls (of Rolls-Royce fame), and other luminaries. Lela's picnic hamper became a popular fixture as the whole family participated in kiting meets.

As the family toured England with *The Klondyke Nugget*, they worked on the kite system whenever they could. The boys became expert kite-system operators. Lela, dressed in her Sunday best, took her first flight with aplomb. As she said later of her husband: "I never knew fear when I was with him. He told me it was safe, so it had to be." She was almost certainly the first woman to fly in a heavier-than-air machine.

Cody's kites were becoming better known than *The Klondyke Nugget*. When playing Glasgow's Metropole Theatre, they flew from the roof, causing traffic jams as everybody in the streets stared at Cody, soaring high above the city. In another incident, murmured stories that a man was flying over the town in a strange machine so disrupted court proceedings in North Shields that the judge ordered a recess. Constables and criminals, along with judge and jury, trooped onto the courthouse steps to see Cody floating high above their town. Cody enjoyed the fame his flying brought him. While the publicity certainly helped his theatrical career, he was coming to see himself more and more as an aviator.

Soon his flying came to the attention of Patrick Alexander, a wealthy experimenter and balloonist, who in 1894 had made parachute jumps from his balloon's basket. Heir to a great fortune, Alexander was fascinated with flight. His wealth enabled him to travel all over the world, visiting most of the handful of early aviation pioneers, from Count Ferdinand von Zeppelin, struggling with engineering his 420-foot rigid airships

Lela takes to the air in her husband's creation, likely the first woman to fly in a heavier-than-air machine.

on Lake Constance in Germany, to Octave Chanute, the famous American engineer who had done pioneering work on glider flying. Alexander had even traveled to Dayton, Ohio, to visit Orville and Wilbur Wright, the foremost experimenters in the United States.

On September 8, 1902, Alexander invited all of England's aviation pioneers to the city of Bath for a hundredth anniversary reenactment of England's first balloon flight.

Unknown to Alexander's guests, that September the Wright brothers were hard at work with their new glider at Kitty Hawk, North Carolina. The gliding performance was much better, but control problems still persisted. All the aviation pioneers struggled with the angles and shapes of wings, as well as control. At this time only the Wrights had figured out that it was necessary to be able to control the airplane so you could point the nose up and down and roll the wingtips up and down, as well as swing the nose from left to right. They had discovered "three-axis" control. With the pilot now free to maneuver in all three axes, or dimensions, it was the breakthrough that made their 1902 glider such a success. In October, they shattered every soaring record in the world with what had become the first truly controllable glider. Whereas Cody had perfected the man-lifting kite, captive to its cable, the Wright brothers had taken the next huge step for heavier-than-air craft, a machine that could be controlled as it flew freely through the air. It would be some time, however, before Chanute brought news of their success to the small band of European pioneers.

Meanwhile, England's lead experimenters were enjoying Alexander's party. Cody was asked to attend and to perform a demonstration of his kites. He built some special lightweight silk kites and prepared other surprises for Alexander's party. The blue-blood enthusiasts attended, including C. S. Rolls and Eric Bruce, one of the founders of Great Britain's Royal Aeronautical Society. Major Trollope was there, along with Baden-Powell and many of Cody's kite-experimenting acquaintances. More important for Cody and British aviation, Colonel Capper, Templer's second-in-command, was in attendance.

Capper, every inch the British Army officer, was also a skilled engineer. At twenty, in 1883, he had built the first British Army balloon under the command of Colonel Templer. He had gone to India, engineering roads and bridges in Kashmir. His engineering had played a major role in the success of balloons in the Boer War, making him a much-decorated hero. The balloons had lifted Army observers high enough so they could accurately direct artillery fire against the enemy. It was rumored that he was to command the prestigious Army Balloon Factory, now operating under his soon-to-retire friend Colonel Templer.

Seemingly a model British officer of the old school, Capper harbored radical ideas. Though he had not yet met Cody, he really believed that people could fly in a powered, controllable, heavier-than-air machine.

The location of the party was not suitable for man-lifting flight, and in any event, Cody had recently survived a near disaster when, with Leon aloft, the winch that controlled the main cable failed in a sudden wind gust. The flailing winch handle had badly broken Cody's arm. It was healing well, but the injury had temporarily halted his man-lifting experiments.

Notwithstanding the broken arm, Cody's display at Alexander's party went flawlessly, the silk kite train floating high above. Smartly dressed in tailored, fringed Western attire, including a large cowboy hat, Cody sent aloft a device that released parachuting fireworks in a striking display, delighting the aviation notables. As Cody winched his kites down, a giant silk "Stars & Stripes"—the American flag—unfurled. The crowd went wild. Alexander called it the *pièce de résistance*, the highlight, of the meeting.

Major Trollope really wanted Colonel Capper to meet Cody. He had a keen sense of both men's obsession with flight. Capper, who had watched Cody from a distance, was as taken aback by Cody's Western regalia as he was intrigued by his kites. But Trollope insisted on making the introduction, pointing out Cody's accomplishments, including his recent feat of taking instruments aloft for the Royal Meteorological Society, over 14,000 feet into the upper atmosphere. Capper was impressed.

Major Trollope was right about Cody and Capper. After the introduction, it took only minutes before the two were deep in flying discussions. It was the start of a lifelong friendship.

The pair talked about Cody's flight with the meteorological instruments, discussing the problems of lifting a huge length of line into the air. Cody described his ingenious winch, which enabled him to reel out three miles of wire and cable. It was based on the wheeled carriage of a large British Army artillery cannon. It was equipped with a brake, a device for measuring

Cody displays a winch with a train of his lifting kites.

social status and had feared that her exuberant husband would run afoul of English class snobbery. At the time, everyone was judged instantly on the way they spoke, and everyone knew the importance of social ranking, from the nobility to the working class. No one could have been more delighted than Lela as she watched her self-made American husband accept the accolades from British scientists and soldiers who saw the value of his work.

In spite of Cody's scientific and military recognition, the War Office bureaucrats still dragged their feet, and the Army High Command seemed determined not to budge. One official even sent Cody a letter saying that the Army had no use for manned flight. Perhaps they could dismiss Cody and his kites, but they didn't reckon on Capper's persistence. They totally missed two paragraphs buried deep in the London *Times*, quietly reporting that on December 7, 1903, Orville and Wilbur Wright had achieved sustained powered flight at Kitty Hawk, North Carolina. For the first time in history, people had built a machine that accelerated under its own power, lifted off the ground, climbed up into the air, sustained its weight on wings, and returned its pilot safely back to earth.

That information had not penetrated the inner workings of the War Office in London. If it had, the logical place for activities such as Cody's would have been at Aldershot, in Hampshire, home of the Army's Balloon Division, with its hangars and large open fields, a mere forty miles southwest of London. Aldershot was the place where Colonel Capper worked, carefully hiding from his skeptical superiors his dreams of heavier-than-air flying machines.

Meanwhile . . . Sparks, Steel, and Structures

It was metal that led the way to the industrial revolution and put Cody and Capper and the Wright brothers on the road to flight. Without strong steel alloy to make bracing wire, reinforcing plates, and engine parts, flight was not possible. Cast iron was too brittle and too heavy. In the three decades before the Civil War, the iron industry had grown by leaps and bounds. But those changes were nothing compared to the revolution that would soon sweep the industry.

Up until the mid-1850s, steel and wrought iron were made in small batches by skilled foundrymen called "puddlers." They would observe the color of the semimolten metal as they turned hundred-pound balls of glowing iron until the carbon oxidized out of the iron and it became steel. When the color of the ball of molten metal "looked right," the batch was done. Steel was so expensive that for decades it was used only on very specific, valuable applications, such as weapons and watch springs. Without the brittleness of the cast iron from which it was made, steel had the springiness and toughness that was essential for strength and light weight.

But in 1855 an Englishman, Henry Bessemer, patented a way of making large batches of steel by blowing air through the molten metal to burn off most of the carbon. It was one of the most spectacular of all industrial processes. The air blew through the molten iron, giving off a huge shower of sparks as metal droplets and carbon showered off the mouth of the converter. However, it still required a skilled opinion to know when the steel was "done." Another Englishman, Robert F. Mushet, discovered that it was possible to burn off all the carbon, then put back just the right amount by adding a recipe of iron, manganese, and carbon. Suddenly iron railroad tracks—which often wore out in two years, were brittle, and could carry only light engines—could be economically replaced with tough, resilient steel strong enough to carry the weight of ever more powerful steam

The Army takes to the air. Cody instructs from horseback at Aldershot.

Like the others, Capper was skeptical of Chanute's latest reports on the Wright brothers, presented at meetings in France and circulated among the aviation enthusiasts. He was somewhat incredulous at their rapid progress. Could they possibly be flying as well as Chanute said? But like most of the small band of aviation enthusiasts, he ultimately respected Chanute, one of the early pioneers of glider experiments, and his reports from America. The committee arranged for Capper to visit America to see the state of developments for himself.

But first, Capper wanted to test Cody's man-lifters at Aldershot. He arranged for Cody and his family to come to the garrison in June and fly from Farnborough Common, near Aldershot, to conduct a full range of tests.

By now, Cody's kite flying had become a theatrical production in its own right. Cody arrived in fringed Western attire complete with a huge white hat, astride his favorite white horse, Bergamo. He led a procession of wagons carrying Lela and the boys, several brightly dressed stagehands from *The Klondyke Nugget*, and all the kite-train equipment and winches. Just as smartly as they changed sets on the stage of *The Klondyke Nugget*, the boys and the stagehands laid out the lines and assembled the kites. Fortunately, it was a good breezy day. Sitting astride Bergamo, Cody directed the operations before an aghast group of men from the Army balloon facility. The Army officers looked on with amazement as Cody and the boys, with stagehands, set up the winch and lofted the kite train. Their reserve gave way to cheers as Cody mounted the man-carrier and soared more than a thousand feet above them. Adjusting the controls, Cody flew effortlessly up and down the line. The officers knew that they could not possibly have used their balloons to conduct artillery observations on such a windy day, and were quick to see just how much Cody had accomplished to be able to control his kites so well.

The performance of the kites fully reinforced Capper's initial judgment of Cody. But Capper really wanted to fly in one of the kites himself that day. Cody was aware that Capper was no stranger to being airborne. He knew that Capper was an enthusiastic amateur balloonist who often took his wife and twelve-year-old daughter flying—amazingly liberal behavior for a Victorian gentleman. Cody felt confident enough of his invention and Capper to permit the additional rider.

In spite of outward calm, Capper climbed into the lifting basket with a sense of real excitement. He watched closely as Cody worked the control lines to adjust the angle of the kite until it lifted them slowly up the line.

"See how I can control the kite angle?" asked Cody. "We're flying on the kite's lift, just like the wings of a bird, not just floating like your hot-air balloons. Here, Capper; you have a go."

Cody passed the control lines to the apprehensive British Army colonel. Determined to execute the task correctly, Capper pulled gently on the line that increased the kite's pitch angle, and they started to climb. He pulled some more. They climbed faster. He decreased the angle carefully, until they stopped climbing. He had control, and he knew it. For a moment, a broad grin spread across Capper's normally reserved visage.

"Okay, Capper, let's try descending. Take it easy—you can get going down way too fast if the wind gets on top of the kite."

They lurched downward, but Capper quickly adjusted the controls. "You're right! It's sensitive when the kite is nearly level with the wind."

Cody was following and feeling Capper's control adjustments. "It's just as bad if you get too steep a climb angle. You get drag on the line, you lose lift, and the kite shakes like mad. It could be really nasty if you lost lift or the front of the kite pitched down too close to the ground."

Cody didn't realize it, but he was talking about the aerodynamics of pitch stability and stall, problems that would plague all the early pioneers of flight—and kill many of them. One of the most frightening prospects even for a modern pilot is loss of pitch control, the ability to control the aircraft at the correct angle to the wind. Without pitch control, an airplane either pitches nose up and falls out of the sky or pitches nose down, plunging to the ground. None of the early pioneers of aviation fully understood the play of forces of air across the

Cody's crew gets ready to assemble a kite train while Cody and an Army officer watch from horseback. Note the chair in front of Cody.

wing, and many found the noses of their crafts rising uncontrollably or plunging down violently, all too often with fatal results.

Developing a safe control system was essential to flight, be it a lighter-than-air balloon, glider, or powered aircraft. It was clear that Cody's kite system had enabled him to safely explore the relationship of pitch control and lift, one of the most dangerous aspects of flight, while safely tethered to the lifting cable. The Wrights had gained exactly the same experience with their hundreds of glider flights, made safely over the sand dunes of Kitty Hawk. Now Capper was even more impressed with the American kite flier. He was more convinced than ever that Cody should come and work with him at Aldershot.

With Capper at the controls, he and Cody slid down the cable to be met by the now totally enthused Army officers awaiting their turns to ascend with Cody.

The rest of the tests went well. Cody even showed what happened when the main cable broke. With ballast in the carrier, the cable was cut. Just as Cody claimed, the kite settled slowly to the ground. "I've had harder balloon landings," said Capper.

His glowing report stated: "I cannot speak too strongly as to the excellence of these kites, their design, and their ability to perform what Mr. Cody claims. . . . Mr. Cody is perhaps the greatest living expert in kite flying, certainly understanding his own kites to an extraordinary degree. . . ." He concluded his report by recommending that the Army purchase Cody's kites and retain him as a kiting instructor.

Satisfied in his judgment of Cody's flying skills and design talents, Capper planned for the time when he would take command of the Balloon Factory. Capper shared with Cody the dream of heavier-than-air flight, and he saw Cody as a vital part of those plans. Capper had to plan diplomatically to make sure he did not offend any of the many factions in the War Office. He had established three goals. The first was to get kite flying fully operational as a means of Army observation, since many influential officers had seen the value of aerial artillery spotting in the Boer War. The second was to complete the design of a powered balloon, which would give the Army the advantage of the tethered observation balloons while also enabling observers to fly over enemy positions. Work on a powered lighter-than-air craft had been started by Colonel Templer, as some officials were worried about other governments—such as the Germans and the French—who were starting to develop powered balloons. Third—an area where Capper was one of a handful of visionaries who saw the potential of powered aircraft—was to start work on designing and building a heavier-than-air craft for the British Army: its first airplane.

Capper was not surprised when Cody told him that he was well along with designing a glider kite that a pilot could control in free flight, much as they had discussed at Alexander's party. He saw his design as a means of learning to fly without the constraints of the kite cable, the next logical step on the road to his vision of soaring freely through the ocean of the air. All the controls would be the same as needed for a powered

Cody demonstrates the kite controls.
The control ropes that enable the man-lifting kite to climb and descend are clearly visible.

airplane. Cody envisioned lifting his glider up the kite cable and then releasing it, much as the Wright brothers had used the steep sand dunes of Kitty Hawk to launch their gliders down the slope. Capper wondered how much progress Cody would make while he was away in America.

Then, armed with introductions from Alexander, Capper was off to the United States on a mission: to see if any of the American flying machines were actually developed enough to be of use to the British Army. He left Cody with orders to start on the design of a powered airship, to be called *Nulli Secundus*, "second to none" in Latin. Cody was to use some of the parts that Templer had acquired when he first started to build an airship.

Capper's visit to America started out poorly. A contest for aeronautics was featured at the St. Louis Exposition, with thousands of dollars in prizes for accomplishing certain goals. While he admired the workmanship of some of the gliders, Capper learned nothing new. He wrote back: "It is a waste of time pointing out anything to an ordinary American. They are all so damned certain they know everything and so absolutely ignorant of the theory of aeronautics that they only resent it."

Capper thought better of the Americans after traveling to Chicago to visit Octave Chanute, well known in the pioneering world of aviation. Chanute had achieved fame and fortune with his engineering during the westward expansion of the railroads in America. Successfully retired, he began studying aeronautics and sponsored sessions of the American Association for the Advancement of Science to promote study of the science of flight. Chanute, raised and educated in Paris, had been a go-between for aviation pioneers on both sides of the Atlantic. He avidly followed all flying experiments in both America and Europe and had financially supported several young pioneers in glider development. He was a friend of the Wrights and had visited them at Kitty Hawk. His articles and reports on their flights had done much to stimulate a new interest in heavier-than-air flight. The scientific community had thought the problems of heavier-than-air flight to be almost insurmountable, especially after Lilienthal's death, and had largely abandoned it in favor of powered balloons.

The pair spent many hours discussing the technology and science of flight. But it was Chanute's two younger friends, the Wright brothers, who were really *flying*. The Wrights' invention of a practical control system had given them mastery of their glider, and enabled them to make their first tentative powered flights. They had achieved this long-sought goal, defined as rising from the ground unassisted, maintaining altitude, and landing again. Capper had to go and see them.

The Wright brothers had become fanatical about maintaining the secrecy of their invention. They were still smarting from a four-day press demonstration in May of that year, where they had barely gotten off the ground. They had written stern letters to their old friend Chanute, insisting that he be careful when writing about their experiments, since premature publication of their ideas on control systems and design of aircraft could scuttle attempts to obtain full patent protection. Indeed, they literally hid their airplane from 1905 to 1908, not flying until they had both patents and a firm deal to sell their design.

On October 24, 1904, Colonel Capper arrived in Dayton, Ohio, to meet Orville and Wilbur Wright. Despite this atmosphere of secrecy and suspicion, Capper and the Wrights struck up an immediate trust and friendship. The Wrights had stopped flying for the year, but—swearing him to secrecy—they showed

Capper their aircraft and flight pictures, something they had done for no one else. They talked candidly of their difficulties and listened with interest to Capper's stories of his experiences with the balloons and the kites.

They talked at length about how control was critical to safe flight. The brothers admitted that they still were working on control problems: the front of the Wright *Flyer*, as they called it, would pitch up or down unpredictably and nearly all their flights in 1904 were short and ended in crashes. But they bravely intended to continue flying until they had the problem solved. Capper urged them to submit a proposal to the War Office in London as soon as they were ready.

They would do so the next year, starting a lengthy correspondence with Capper that continued the friendship. Capper's reports to the committee and Army engineers were candid in their admiration of the Wrights and their accomplishments.

Meantime, his American mission completed, Capper had to return to his duties at the Balloon Factory in Aldershot to see whether he could move matters there forward faster.

CHAPTER 6

SECOND TO NONE?

Capper returned to Aldershot to find Cody well underway in setting up a training program for the Army so it could have experienced kite crews for artillery spotting. Work was nearly done on the glider kite, and an ingenious design was completed for the mechanics and controls of the airship *Nulli Secundus*. Capper was more determined than ever that Cody should be a permanent part of the Balloon Factory.

So Cody was starting on yet another adventure, under a long-term contract arranged by Capper, which gave him the rights of an Army officer and the title of Chief Kite Instructor. Cody's heart was no longer in the theater. This was the chance to follow his dream of flight. So closing the book on *The Klondyke Nugget*, Cody and Lela gave up their nomadic lives and settled in Aldershot, England. Leon and Vivian, now in their mid-twenties, came to work with Cody at the Balloon Factory. Frank, much younger, still had to attend school, but he helped when he could.

Cody, with Capper's blessing, let his sons do much of the kite instruction, while Cody pushed ahead with the powered balloon, the airship *Nulli Secundus*. Work progressed rapidly on a "spine" to

The drive unit for the *Nulli Secundus* sits in front of the Balloon shed. The balloon envelope can be seen inflated in the hangar.

be suspended under the balloon to distribute the loads of the engine, with its twin propellers, wings, controls, and passengers, along the length of the soft balloon envelope. The only material that could contain the fine hydrogen molecules was "goldbeater's skin," made from the linings of cows' stomachs. It was so costly that Colonel Templer, Capper's mentor and predecessor, had spent virtually his entire budget on the balloon envelope, now to be used for the *Nulli Secundus*.

The glider kite was finished and already flying. Looking a little like a giant version of the wings on the man-lifting kites, it was far more a kite than an airplane. Its wings were of stretched canvas like a kite, not the efficiently curved airfoil shapes of the Wright brothers' very successful glider. To make up for its inefficiency, it was even bigger than the Wrights' glider. It had a wingspan of 51 feet, an area of 807 square feet, and it weighed (without a pilot) 116 pounds. More important, like the Wrights, Cody had recognized that it was essential to be able to control the glider in any direction. Cody had designed a clever system of movable surfaces on the trailing edge of the wings. While Cody's design was not as sophisticated as the Wrights' glider, it still gave the pilot control in all three axes: pitch (nose up/nose down), roll (wingtip up/down), and yaw (nose side to side). Soon after its first flights it also sported a stabilizing tail that made it more stable and easy to control, much like the tail on a kite. To launch the glider, Cody climbed aboard a canvas sling mounted on the lower wing, then flew the glider up the kite-train cable, just as he did with his man-lifting kite. Then he would slide forward in the canvas sling until the glider's nose tilted down and it released from the cable, descending in free flight.

Cody supervises soldiers in the assembly of the glider kite.

Vivian made the longest flight of 740 feet from a height of 300 feet. Performance with Cody's 200-plus pounds was less impressive, but it gave him the valuable experience he knew he needed in controlling an aircraft in all three axes, a vital bridge to be crossed on the road to powered flight. Cody had long understood the danger of merely powering a flying machine without an ability to keep it flying straight and level in turbulent air, a fact that many early experimenters ignored at their peril. As the Wright brothers had told Capper, control was life itself!

After a few modifications, the glider became easy to fly, and many Army officers being trained on kites also flew it. While there was not much apparent military value, it was great, exciting fun. In every sense of the word, it was the first true hang glider—and started a sport of recreational flying that exists to this day.

An Army officer pilots the glider at Aldershot.

Yet even though Cody designed the glider with a large wing area and incorporated controls to keep the wings level without weight shifting, his son Vivian was severely injured when, flying on a gusty day in September 1905, he lost pitch control; the nose reared up and the glider fell and slid sideways, hitting the ground almost too fast for survival of the pilot.

The accident appeared almost identical to the Wrights' experience, when Orville had a near-disastrous crash on September 13, 1902. Learning to fly at Kitty Hawk, his brother yelling instructions from the ground, Orville had let the aircraft nose up too high, and it, too, stalled and slid sideways and backward into the ground. Orville ended up in a "heap of flying machine, cloth, and sticks in a heap, me in the center without a scratch or bruise."

Cody did not rebuild his glider since he was already underway on his next design and was completing work on the powered airship, *Nulli Secundus*.

This new design was another bridge between the kites and powered flight. Cody developed an unmanned aircraft powered by one of a pair of twelve-horsepower three-cylinder French engines owned by the Balloon Factory and used in its experiments. Cody had done exactly what he had discussed with Capper on their first meeting: he mounted the engine on a version of his kites, adding an undercarriage and tail booms with fins for stability. Little is known of the tests of this "model" aircraft, but it was a success, flying with stability and convincing Capper that

A glider crash. Not all the landings were successful.

Cody was on the right track. Now all they had to do was design a large enough airplane to carry the weight of pilot and engine, work out a control system, and, more important, learn to fly! While the experience with the kites and the glider was invaluable, powered flight would be venturing into an unknown realm.

Delighted with the progress, Capper sent Cody to the December 1906 Paris Auto Show to find the best engine for the nearly completed *Nulli Secundus*. He purchased a French Antoinette that, although it performed well, was hard to start. Cody replaced the engine's small flywheel with a larger, spoked wheel that he pulled on to start the engine. Cody was the only man at the Balloon Factory strong enough to spin the engine fast enough for the magnetos in the engine to fire the spark plugs and bring it to life.

Another step on the road to flight. The unmanned aircraft in the Balloon shed.

Cloaked in secrecy at the Balloon Factory, the *Nulli Secundus* progressed rapidly. Working at all hours, Cody and his sons designed, formed, machined, and assembled the parts of the airship. Word had leaked out that Count von Zeppelin had made long, successful flights in his new powered airship carrying passengers. Von Zeppelin had decided that the best way to build an airship was to make a rigid frame out of aluminum. Gas bags inside the streamlined frame were filled with lighter-than-air helium or hydrogen to provide lift. The rigid frame allowed this aircraft to carry much stronger engines. Von Zeppelin's 420-foot-long monster was much faster than a simple powered balloon and could fly in much stronger winds and bad weather. Soon the count's name became synonymous with the rigid airships. The military potential was obvious. The zeppelin could fly unopposed over enemy territory, observing, carrying troops, or dropping bombs.

German militarism, which soon fueled World War I, emerged in statements from the German privy councilor. He boasted that Germany would build a fleet of thousands of zeppelins, each carrying twenty soldiers, "which would land and capture the sleeping Britons before they could realize what was happening."

The French were also having some success with powered balloons and were extolling the military virtues of aerial navigation for directing artillery, spotting troop movements, and dropping firebombs on an enemy. Many in the British government saw the threat. Though the War Office downplayed it, it still put pressure on Capper to do something with his meager budget.

On September 9, 1907, the *Nulli Secundus* floated out from the huge Balloon Factory shed, carefully controlled by dozens of soldiers holding on to ropes. Carrying Cody, Colonel Capper, and another Balloon Factory officer, Captain King, the new

Burton Haldane. Haldane viewed Cody, Capper, Dunne, and the Wrights all as clever amateurs. He was genuinely concerned about the zeppelin threat and admired the "scientific" approach of Germany's expensive, government-supported project. A master politician, he set the wheels in motion to remove "the amateurs."

The *Nulli Secundus,* just before lifting off.

If Haldane had his way, all of Capper and Cody's work would come to nothing, and all research into flight by the Army would be halted. Colonel Capper needed to do something spectacular in a hurry. He launched an impetuous plan that would, if unsuccessful, end not only the Army's flight experiments but also his own career. He turned to Cody and the *Nulli Secundus*. Early on the morning of October 10, 1907, Cody and Capper met at the Balloon Factory shed. "Well, Cody, you appear to have everything in hand. It seems the airship will keep flying as long as we have fuel on board," said Capper.

Cody had worked on the chain drives for the propellers and improved the airship's controls so that he could control the height with them, rather than by dumping sand ballast and venting gas. Cody told Capper that he felt confident the machine could fly for as long as its fuel lasted, up to several hours.

Standing at the door of the Balloon Factory in full regimental uniform, Capper looked at Cody, up at the airship, then back at Cody. He made an instant decision. "Right. We shall fly to London, now." The city lay forty miles away. The *Nulli Secundus* had never flown more than a few miles from Farnborough, near Aldershot. No one in England had yet dreamed of flying that far. For once, Cody was the one taken aback, but only for a moment.

One problem remained. The Balloon Factory did not have a vehicle that could keep pace with the airship so the Royal Engineers soldiers (called Sappers) could keep up and help, should the need arise. Cody smiled and offered to lend his new car, one of the first at Aldershot. Cody said they could leave right away, as long as they flew over his house so he could yell down to Lela that he wouldn't be home for lunch. Cody grabbed a clean motoring coat, and Capper got some message streamers so he could drop them to the soldiers in the car below.

At 10:30 A.M., the *Nulli Secundus* was airborne and a few minutes later was circling Cody's house as he yelled his message to Lela. Then the airship roared off several hundred feet above the road to London. Its speed of 16 miles per hour was raised to a blistering 25 miles per hour by a brisk breeze from behind. Cody had brought along a Klaxon air horn, which he honked enthusiastically as they passed over small towns on their way to the city.

The Sappers pursued them, managing to stay beneath the airship most of the way. At Brentwood, a streamer plummeted down. The message read: "We shall enter the city and attempt to circle St. Paul's. Keep close, in case of emergency." The airship was behaving perfectly and London lay beneath them in golden autumn sunshine. Ahead was Hyde Park; beyond it, Buckingham Palace.

"Cody, I'm going to fly low over the palace gardens. The king said we could land there next week for his inspection if we really are 'second to none.' I want to reconnoiter," Capper announced.

Cody voiced caution: "The breeze is picking up. Let's take a look—the air might get pretty rough near the ground."

"Right, and Cody, please don't blow that damned Klaxon at the palace."

"Okay, Colonel." Cody could hardly conceal his smile.

The *Nulli Secundus* slowed and lowered to treetop height in the palace garden, nodding up and down in the breeze spilling over the trees. Many onlookers thought the airship was "saluting" the palace. People crowded into parks and onto rooftops to watch. London traffic came to a halt at the novel sight of the airship plowing through the skies over London.

Thousands ran into the streets of London as the *Nulli Secundus* flew overhead.

THERE'LL ALWAYS BE AN ENGLAND

CHAPTER 7

All England was ecstatic about Cody's flight.

For the rest of October 1907, every newspaper, magazine, and journal in the land carried articles, pictures, poems, and artwork on Cody, Capper, and the *Nulli Secundus*. Even the military establishment was pleased with the flight. It gave them something to point to as the Army's response to the growing rumors of the "zeppelin menace." They even supported Cody and Capper's vision of powered, heavier-than-air flight, authorizing a small expenditure of £50 (a couple of hundred dollars in today's money) to design *Army Airplane #1*! That was all that Cody and Capper needed—they wasted not a second in getting started.

Capper's specifications for the airplane were military and ambitious. It would be able to carry two 170-pound crew members, have a cruising speed of at least 25 miles per hour, reach an altitude of 2,000 feet with a full load, and be capable of operating from rough ground, a condition that certainly existed at the Balloon Factory's home on Farnborough Common. It would be usable for observation, carrying dispatches, and dropping munitions.

Cody quickly sketched a design and started fabrication in the Balloon Factory shed under conditions of strictest secrecy. The aircraft was to have

Stitching the fabric on the wings of the airplane. Army wives helped as Cody supervised.

a span of 52 feet, a length of 44 feet, and a wing area of 857 square feet, and weigh just over a ton when ready to fly. In contrast, the Wright *Flyer* had a span of 41 feet, had 520 square feet of wing area, had a flying weight of 625 pounds, and would take off only from a wheeled carriage that rolled down a dead-smooth rail laid directly into the wind.

The rough ground around Aldershot required rugged construction. Cody provided a strong coiled-spring suspension with wheels at the nose, tail, and wingtips to absorb shock and prevent the structure from catching on the humps and hillocks of Farnborough Common.

Work on the plane progressed rapidly, but the vast amount of stitching on the wing covering impeded progress. Leon and Vivian were swamped with sewing, despite their skills with sewing machines. Lela came up with a solution. Friendly with many Balloon School wives, she enlisted their help to sew the wing coverings for the new craft. Even the aristocratic Mrs. Capper pitched in. Her daughter, Edith, who still went hot-air ballooning with her father, commented that she had never seen her mother working before!

The airplane stood on its nose in the Balloon shed as the work went on.

Cody claimed that Lela, or rather her cooking, solved another important design issue. The fabric on the wings had to be sized (sealed and stiffened). Varnish was useless if the fabric got damp, and development of aircraft "dope," the special flexible paint used to size the covering fabric, was still four years in the future. But Cody noticed the stiff, starchy texture of Lela's tapioca pudding. A quick test of the tapioca liquid on a test around the common. One journalist commented that it was "a mere taxi." Cody ignored them and went on with his work.

Finally, in May 1908, Cody and his sons had achieved sufficient balance that the aircraft could accept full throttle and still be controllable in pitch as it accelerated. Cody held the nose dead stable, and as the airplane went faster, the rumbling of the undercarriage stopped. Carefully he reduced the throttle until he once again felt the vibration of the wheels on the ground. The boys were jumping up and down, waving and yelling at him. They had seen lots of daylight under the wheels! They looked at the tracks in the grass. The aircraft had left the ground for hundreds of feet. They were ready to really fly in a heavier-than-air, engine-powered machine!

~ Meanwhile . . . Power, Performance, and Perfume ~

Powered flight demanded motors of small size, light weight, and high efficiency. Engineers had long sought a way to replace the steam engine and its massive boiler. To scientists and engineers, the idea of injecting something explosive into a cylinder and setting it off to push the piston and turn the crankshaft was a pretty obvious idea. Getting it to work was anything but easy.

In 1860, Etienne Lenoir invented the spark ignition, and soon engines run on natural gas became common for the powering of machinery in small shops. By using an electric spark to ignite the gas at just the right time, the force of the explosion pushed the piston down, generating power. Lenoir's invention evolved into the modern spark plug that all gasoline engines use today. The newfangled electricity also drove demand for more efficient engines. The advent of small engines that could be turned on and off was a boon to the small workshop. Soon, primitive gasoline engines, sometimes called "make and break" or "spit and hope" engines after their ignition magnetos and fuel systems, became common. The Wright brothers built their own gasoline engine to power their shop and wind tunnel.

These engines, while very useful, were heavy and inefficient. They were mostly what are called two-stroke engines. Their pistons went up, sucking in fuel and air and squeezing it. Then the spark plug exploded the fuel, pushing the piston down. Thus, two strokes completed the power cycle. However, in 1876, N. A. Otto came up with a way to make an engine with a four-stroke cycle. One down stroke sucked the fuel and air into the cylinder, the next up stroke compressed it; with the third stroke the fuel was ignited and pushed the piston down, and a final upstroke pushed the burned gases down the exhaust pipe. The four-stroke "Otto" cycle was vastly more efficient. Otto proposed a vehicle called the Otto-Mobile. The name would catch on, even if the spelling didn't.

Sailors look at the engineless airplane.

diminishes rapidly with altitude. Santos-Dumont's crude design could never climb any higher.

Most modern aircraft have flaps or ways to increase drag (resistance to moving through the air); modern sailplanes and jetliners have "spoilers" atop the wings to kill lift. If they did not, ground effect would make them float off the far end of even the longest runways. These ground-effect "cushioning" phenomena are why many scientists say that the 1905 Wright *Flyer* was the first true airplane: photos show it flying well out of ground effect, several wingspans above the ground.

But these first stumbling flights electrified France. On November 18, 1907, Orville Wright was at Issy, near Paris, when Henri Farman staggered aloft in his airplane with just rudder and elevator for pitch control—and without roll control. He skidded around a one-kilometer course, just barely above the ground, trying to win the Deutsch-Archdeacon prize for the first circular flight. He did not win that day—the judges ruled that he had not properly closed the circle and one of his wheels had touched the ground while turning. He finally succeeded the following January.

Reporters flocked to the Wrights, who were there to finalize negotiations with their French licensees. Orville said that he and his brother "never liked to pass criticism on others' work . . . time will tell whether the Farman machine's controls are adequate to meet the conditions encountered in windy weather."

But Ernest Archdeacon, a senior member of the French flying community, spoke for many in Europe when he said: "The famous Wright brothers may today claim all they wish. If it is true—and I doubt it more and more—that they were the first to fly through the air [in 1903], they will not have the glory before history. They would only have had to eschew these incomprehensible affectations of mystery and carry out their experiments in the broad daylight, like Santos-Dumont and Farman, and before official judges, surrounded by thousands of spectators. The first *authentic* experiments in powered aviation have taken place in France; and the famous fifty kilometers announced by the Wrights will, I am sure, be beaten by us as well before they will have decided to show their phantom machine."

The rebuilt *Nulli Secundus* used the only engine available to Cody, frustrating his tests of the airplane.

Cody spent a summer of total frustration shuttling between Navy tests and the Balloon Factory, watching the only engine available to him flailing around in the lighter-than-air airship, the *Nulli Secundus the Second*, as it floated around in a series of unsuccessful tests. Through no fault of his own or his design, he was effectively grounded.

And the Wrights were about to change everything.

At 6 P.M., on August 8, 1908, Wilbur launched their airplane, the Wright *Flyer*, on a test flight from the race track at Les Hunaudieres, near Le Mans, France. He soared up in an effortless sweeping turn, circled the track twice, and descended gracefully, almost exactly at his takeoff point. It was all over in two minutes.

Only a few observers were in the grandstands, but Ernest Archdeacon and Louis Blériot were among them. They had been waiting for days, perhaps hoping to see "*les bluffeurs*" (as they called them) get their comeuppance. But they knew the significance of what they had seen: the upward swoop, the steeply banked turns, the graceful descent. The French fliers were merely paddling in the shallows; the Wrights had clearly mastered the ocean of the air.

The next day, Archdeacon published a gracious apology for his earlier comments. "For a long time, too long a time, the

Wright brothers have been accused in Europe of bluff—even perhaps in the land of their birth. They are today hallowed in France, and I feel an intense pleasure in counting myself among the first to make amends for that flagrant injustice."

Cody and Capper and the entire European aviation community were in turmoil. While there had been many rumors about the Wrights and the performance of their machine, no one was prepared for their absolute supremacy and the practical utility of their airplane. Only weeks before, the Army Chief of Staff and Secretary of State for War Haldane had assured the prime minister and the public that balloons, zeppelins, and airplanes would not threaten England's security for the foreseeable future. Yet here were the French, extolling the military virtues of dropping incendiary bombs from fleets of Wright *Flyers*! World War I and the first dropping of bombs from zeppelins on a civilian population were only six years into the future.

Poor Capper had virtually no room to do anything to meet the demands for a British airplane. He grounded the airship, allowing Cody to install the tired Antoinette in *Army Airplane #1*. Between trips to Portsmouth for the Navy, Cody supervised his sons in reinstalling the engine in his airplane, which they

The first sustained powered flight in England . . .

"freshened up" as much as possible, installing new radiators.

On September 28, 1908, Cody took the airplane for more tests. Moving the radiators had changed the balance, so Cody did not attempt to fly. The press, seeking spectacular events, were disappointed, and commented snidely that Cody was just "driving the airplane round the common like a car." Cody directed the boys to make more changes.

Returning on October 9, Cody tested the modified airplane. Finding control much improved, he lifted the wheels a little way off the ground and made a few short hops. The press saw no significant improvement from the experiments of that spring, and the contemptuous reporting increased, with reference to Britain's "grasshopper airplane" and its Yankee showman pilot. Capper tried to keep the press at bay, explaining that Cody was not yet expected to fly, but the press was having none of that. Cody gritted his teeth and went on with his tests.

Finally, on October 9, Cody lifted off the ground a few feet with good, solid pitch control. He could hold the nose steady, with no pitching up or down. He was nearly ready.

On October 13, after a particularly vicious round of attacks in the press, Cody finished his day's tests by roaring down on the group of reporters standing between him and the Balloon Factory, lifting off and flying a few feet over their heads. The *Daily Mirror* published a picture. Capper was livid at Cody for risking the airplane, and at the *Daily Mirror* for publishing the photograph. Now, all chance of preserving secrecy was lost. Capper had hoped that he could let Cody conduct all the early flights in private, away from the pressures to fly before he was ready. The *Daily Mirror* and other papers now assigned reporters to watch the Balloon Factory around the clock.

On October 16, astute observers noticed a British flag tied to the strut behind the pilot as the airplane was wheeled out of the Balloon Factory shed. Cody had made minor wing changes, changing the camber (curve of the wing) to improve pitch stability and reduce drag. It was just over nine weeks after the Wrights' first historic public flights in France.

Cody made his usual high-speed taxiing tests. Starting up the hill to the Swann Inn plateau above the common, he advanced the throttle and *flew up the hill,* landing at the top.

Cody carefully turned the airplane so that he was looking downhill at Cove Common. After a last check that the field was clear and the wind was coming from dead ahead, he slowly but purposefully advanced the throttle. The plane surged ahead.

Listening carefully to make sure that the engine was up to speed, Cody pulled back on the control wheel to gently raise the nose a few degrees. Soon the aircraft was balanced on its wheels, accelerating rapidly, almost ready to fly.

Holding the nose at exactly the right angle, Cody let the airplane continue to accelerate. The rumbling of the wheels stopped abruptly as they left the ground, the aircraft sliding up an invisible ramp in the air.

Keeping the control movements small and the nose pointing at the same spot on the horizon, Cody allowed the aircraft to continue to climb. Still climbing, he felt a difference in pressure on the control wheel.

Overcorrecting, the airplane zoomed upward, slowing dangerously. Bravely, realizing that he couldn't afford to overcontrol, Cody released just a little pressure on the controls, allowing the nose to lower, waiting, his heart in his mouth, as the aircraft accelerated again to a safe speed.

By now he was flying well above the roof of the giant Balloon shed, more than fifty feet in the air, far higher than he intended. But the airplane was flying well; Cody was making little movements with the controls to keep it balanced and flying level.

With the barest moment to relax and look around, he realized that he had flown far too high to land at his intended spot. He did not want to abruptly push the nose down to reach it, since he was still learning the feel of the controls.

So he climbed a little to clear a clump of trees ahead of him and land beyond them. He eased back on the control wheel and cleared them easily, only to be jerked about by the turbulence of the breeze passing over them. Regaining balance, Cody saw that the turbulence had pointed him toward a shrub- and tree-covered part of the common, where he could not possibly land safely.

Cody turned his aircraft abruptly back to the level area beyond the trees, but the aircraft responded far more quickly than it had on the ground. One wing raised up, Cody wrestled to get the plane level again, but it slowed and started falling sideways toward the ground. There was nothing that Cody could do.

. . . and the results of the first landing.

Vivian, in the white coat, inspects the scene of the crash.

Crunch!

The airplane slid sideways into the ground, the collision smashing the left wingtip wheel, pivoting the aircraft violently, and splintering the lower-left wing panel. Cody shut down the still-spinning engine and emerged from the wreckage. He looked back at the Balloon Factory shed, over a quarter mile away. He had been airborne nearly half a minute.

Cody had made the first sustained powered flight in England.

FLIERS OR LIARS?

CHAPTER 9

Cody had flown 1,390 feet in a powered, heavier-than-air machine. What had he accomplished? What did his flight mean? In the plainest possible terms, Cody had learned how to fly. It is clear that only the pioneers themselves knew the extraordinary difficulty of their task. Cody had accomplished so much, yet it was far from the popular images of the fantasy of flight. Both Cody and the Wrights would suffer from this lack of appreciation for their accomplishments.

Even though the popular press had been full of tales of marvelous flying machines, the public had been suspicious of these claims. On February 10, 1906, the *New York Herald,* in an editorial headlined "Fliers or Liars," had concluded that nothing had been proven about flight or who could really fly: "The Wrights have either flown or have not flown. They either possess a machine or do not possess one. They are either fliers or liars. It is difficult to fly. It is easy to say: 'We have flown.'"

It is unlikely that the *Herald* knew how difficult it really was to fly. News reporting was, if anything, less accurate than today. Many people had made extravagant claims of prodigious flying feats, often reported in print.

At the 1903 St. Louis Exposition, which Capper had attended, Wilbur Wright had commented that those seeking the $100,000 main flight prize might have better luck with an alternate means of propulsion. In a letter to Chanute he wrote: "Mule power might have greater ascensional force if properly applied, but I fear it would be dangerous unless the mule wore pneumatic shoes." Referring to newspaper accounts of his competitors, he concluded: "Some of these reports would disgust one if they were not so irresistibly ludicrous."

As the *New York Herald* stated, it was easy to say: "We have flown." In spite of the many extravagant claims of the time, history would later show that by 1908, *only five humans* had acquired any significant time operating heavier-than-air flying machines—and two of them were dead. Otto Lilienthal and Percy Pilcher, a Scottish engineer who had studied with him, had been killed in flying accidents. Samuel Cody and the Wrights were the only ones who had more than brief seconds in heavier-than-air flight—the Wrights with their gliders, Cody with his kites and glider and hours of taxiing tests and short hops in his airplane on Laffan's Plain. In all the other claims, no one knew enough to ask the vital question: "How did you learn to fly?"

In France in 1909, Wilbur Wright and his sister Katharine prepare for a flight as Orville looks on. Modesty dictated that the skirts of female passengers be tied, and this actually started a fashion craze for "hobble" skirts.

The crafts of Pilcher and Lilienthal had proven to be killers; Cody and the Wright brothers all had narrow escapes. In many cases, only the fact that the Wrights were flying their glider over gently sloping sand into a strong headwind, which limited their speed over the ground, prevented serious or fatal crashes. Cody learned control in pitch by "flying" his lifting kite up and down the line, varying the angle of the kite, and getting a feel for the lift: knowledge he later used in his free-flying kite glider and in his airplane.

Pitch control was the biggest killer. It killed Lilienthal when, on August 9, 1896, at the Rhinow Hills, his glider pitched up and he fell out of the sky. He died the next day at a hospital in Berlin. His last words were "Sacrifices must be made." It took Pilcher's life in 1899 when his aircraft nosed up suddenly, the poorly understood loads of the wind on the wings folding them up and plummeting Pilcher to earth.

As late as 1905, the Wright brothers had found that they were losing pitch control, a problem that caused their most serious crash on July 14. The Wrights had always feared a serious crash from loss of control, and this was it. The aircraft started a series of up-down oscillations in which Orville finally lost control and plunged straight into the ground at 30 miles per hour.

He was flung into the forward elevator; the upper-wing main spar smashed down across his back. Incredibly, the crash had already broken the spar exactly where it hit him or it would have crushed his spine and killed him. As it was, he survived, dazed and badly bruised. Living long enough to learn to fly involved luck, too.

Perhaps learning to fly was best described by Wilbur in his speech to a group of Chicago engineers in 1901, where he described the Wrights' glider experiments: "There are two ways of learning how to ride a fractious horse. One is to get on him and learn by actual practice how each motion and trick may best be met; the other is to sit on a fence and watch the beast a while, then retire to the house and leisurely figure out the best way of overcoming his jumps and kicks.

"The latter system is safer but the former, on the whole, turns out more good riders. It is much the same learning to ride a flying machine; if you are looking for perfect safety, you will do well to sit on a fence and watch the birds; but if you really wish to learn, you must mount a machine and become acquainted with its tricks by actual trial."

Kite flying was a valuable test method for Orville and Wilbur. Here, they fly their 1902 *Glider* as a kite, just as Cody would do with his glider kite.

It is no coincidence that Cody, too, looked at riding an airplane much like riding a horse. Like the Wrights, he talked of "riding" the aircraft, rather than steering it as a ship across an ocean. He knew the risks of losing pitch control and of lateral instability with his kites. He had to solve control problems with his free-flying kite glider.

The courage of Cody and the Wrights in approaching the unknown areas of flight can only be marveled at. They knew that the only way to learn was to take risks that might kill them.

Cody's accomplishment was enormous. He had built an airplane that let him take off unassisted over rough ground (a

Cody ponders his next test flight.

handicap the Wrights, using a catapult launch, didn't face). His aircraft could take off repeatedly, fly straight ahead, make gentle turns, and land again. But he, more than anyone else except Orville and Wilbur, knew how much more risk and experiment would be necessary before he truly mastered the air. He could not tell if his problems with sharper turns were something within the aircraft or in his piloting. He set about finding out.

Meanwhile . . . One Good Turn . . .

Follow the Cody *Flyer* to see how hard it was for the first plane to make a successful turn. After all, the first fliers were instructor, student, and test pilot all at once, especially on the first few flights. The arrows show which controls are moving. The aileron on either wingtip rolls the wingtips up or down. The elevator at the front moves the nose up and down in pitch, and the rudders at the back yaw the nose left or right. It was the Wrights who first discovered that the secret of flight was to control the aircraft in all three directions: roll, pitch, and yaw. Both Cody and the Wrights crashed a lot before they learned to turn. It was not like riding a bicycle, where you could get back on again before you thought about it too much. You had to fix your airplane, which often took weeks, think very hard about why it crashed the first time, and go up into the sky and try again. The first pilots were very brave.

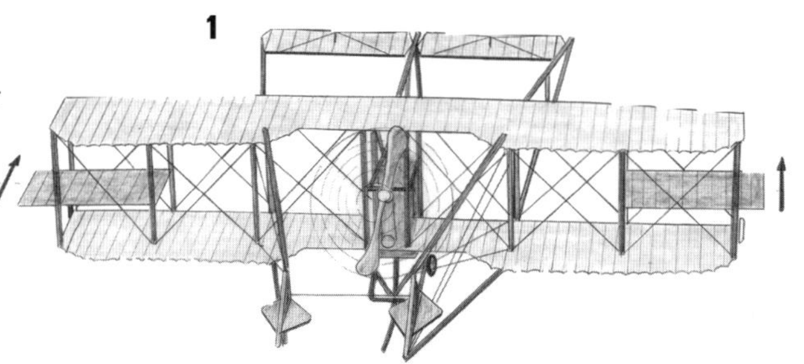

1
Okay, you're straight and level, and you've just figured out how to keep the airplane at the right height.

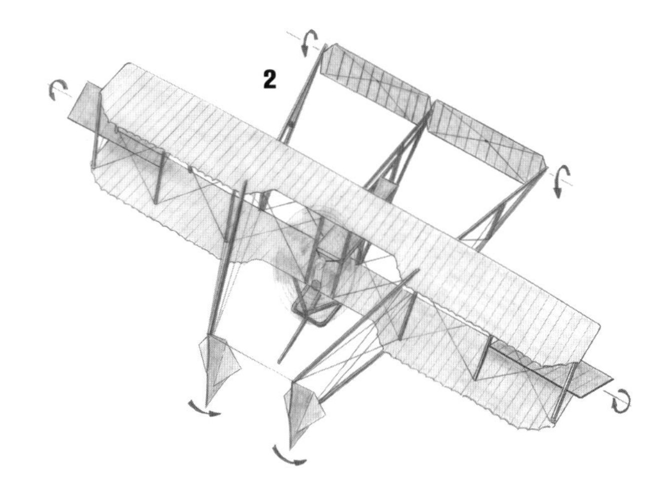

2
Just like Cody, start your very first turn in the air. Feed in a little rudder to move the nose right. Add a little aileron to bank the airplane, or it will just skid sideways. Not too much, or the airplane will slip to the inside of the turn. If you're too low, the right wingtip will hit the ground. Whoooo! As you add aileron, the nose wants to go LEFT. If you make the wing lift more, it drags more, so the left wing is trying to pull the nose left! Feed in more right rudder! The nose moving the wrong way is called "adverse yaw." Feed some up-elevator to keep your altitude because you need more lift in a turn.

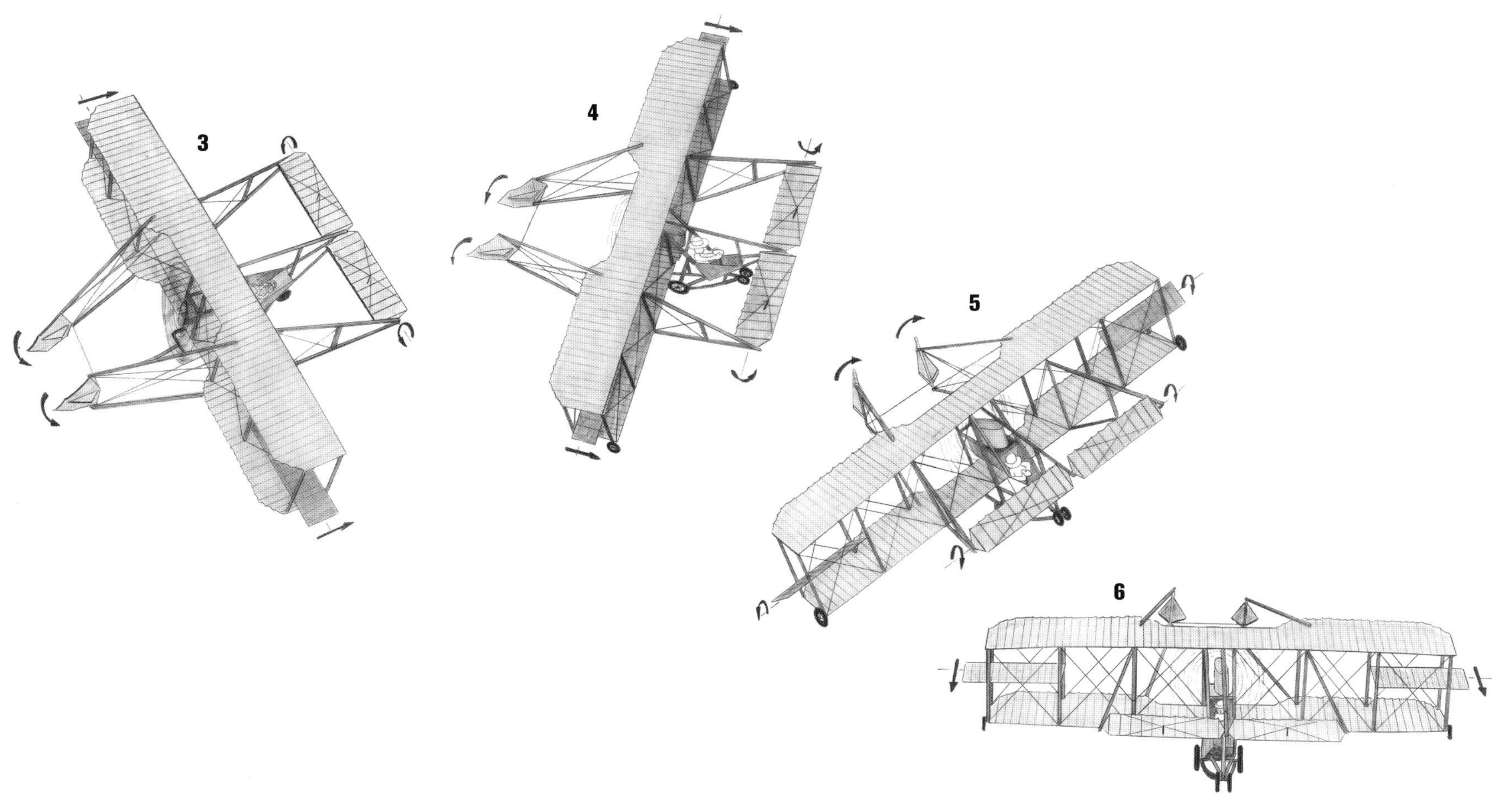

3

Feed in some right aileron to stop the airplane banking too much and make small adjustments with the rudder and elevator to keep the turn smooth and coordinated. The early airplanes were upset by even the slightest gusts of wind, and the pilot would have to react quickly with ailerons, elevator, and rudder to avoid a crash.

4

Hopefully, the airplane is fairly stable and you only have to make small corrections to keep it turning smoothly. Modern airplanes want to fly straight and level and are easy to control in gentle turns. The early airplanes were anything but, and even the Wright brothers crashed repeatedly as they worked to balance their controls.

5

Time to stop the turn. Apply aileron to roll the aircraft to the left, feed in a little left rudder, and ease the nose down, as you don't need as much lift as the aircraft levels out.

6

Congratulations: straight and level again. Ready for your very first landing?

wings, making it visible. He flew successfully more than a quarter mile, but when he tried to turn sharply, the front rudder (or elevator) failed and folded back over the top wing. Fortunately, Cody was unhurt in the descent, the plane only slightly damaged. And Cody gained some valuable lessons. The streamers not only showed him how to improve airflow over the wings but gave him vital control clues.

He could now tell when the airplane was flying straight relative to the wind or at an angle to it. If he kept the streamers straight back, the plane was balanced, even in a turn. If they were off to one side, he was slipping or skidding, creating drag the puny Antoinette engine could not overcome. He knew now for certain that the first crash had been caused by his overcontrol of the aircraft. As long as he manipulated the controls so the streamers blew straight back over the wings, the airplane would not slip or skid but would turn in a coordinated manner. He told Capper he would soon master the problem of banking for turns (thinking of the banking on racetracks, such as the famous one at Brooklands).

. . . Cody repeats the test, with the streamers untied, as he flies past a group of observers.

Capper's frustration shows in a report on the incident. By now, Capper (at his own expense) had visited France, along with many other aviation enthusiasts. In a report to the War Office, Capper wrote: "I myself am of the opinion, as I told him [Cody] before, that his front rudder [elevator] is unnecessarily large, in fact dangerously so. I shall advise Mr. Cody to use a smaller front rudder, but as the design is entirely his own—though I make suggestions at times—it rests entirely with him whether he follows my advice or not."

Negative press about "grasshopper airman," "lawn mowing again," "agricultural machinery," and "taxi" continued.

On February 18, 1909, Cody flew successfully but blew a tire on landing. On February 23, while determining the slowest speed at which he could maintain control, the "airplane seemed to stop still in midair, then fell to the ground." Cody had just discovered stalling—what happens when an airplane is going too slowly and the airflow over the wing can't generate lift and becomes turbulent. But only minor damage resulted, and another important lesson was learned.

Cody's shed at Laffan's Plain, with the rebuilt aircraft standing outside.

The next day, Cody flew all over Laffan's Plain, turning left and right, taking off and landing at will. He ended with a long, straight, quarter-mile flight back to the Balloon Factory shed "really to convince the press that my reckless maneuvering was intentional and that the machine was completely under control."

It was to no avail. The negative press and Secretary of State for War Haldane prevailed. Despite having met the Wrights and Capper, Haldane dismissed them as merely "clever empiricists" and found Cody and the Balloon Factory programs "an embarrassment." Voting to provide small funds to the Army and Navy for airship work, he canceled all aircraft programs, claiming the Army could buy aircraft commercially, should they ever prove practical.

The day after Cody had finally demonstrated mastery of his craft, he received a letter from the War Office. It read: "I am commanded by the Army Council to inform you that, in view of changes contemplated in connection with balloons and flying machines, it has been decided to terminate the engagements of Lt. Dunne and Mr. S. F. Cody." The letter was signed R. H. Brade, Assistant Secretary for War. It was a bitter blow for Cody, just when his dreams of flight were within reach. Adding insult to injury, the Army was still stonewalling his efforts to get it to honor its commitments on his kite patent applications.

The press had a field day, with comments and captions like: "Cody's farewell. God Save the Taxpayer. We could not love you, sir, so much, loved we not money more. It will be hoped that the authorities will now finance an ENGLISHMAN'S experiments."

The respected *Westminster Gazette* took a broader view of Cody's firing. The editor wrote:

> It has evidently perturbed many people that an ex-cowboy should have broken down the social barriers in this country by securing an appointment in His Majesty's Army. Nor do they seem to have forgotten that the intrepid aviator was once a showman. They seem to imagine that he has bluffed the War Office into giving him an appointment in which he could enjoy all the sweets and emoluments of a "soft" job and live voluptuously at taxpayer's expense. . . .
>
> It is easy to sit in one's armchair and ask why Mr.

Cody's flights became so routine that no one at Aldershot paid too much attention, even the cows.

> Cody has done this, that and the other thing, but those who talk most can usually do the least. Mr. Cody has done quite as much and a good deal more with his airplane than the majority of Continental aviators. Mr. Cody has been made the butt for all the errors that should rightly be laid against the War Office. . . . It is a great pity that Mr. Cody should be deprived of his appointment just when his ideas may be of great value to the nation.

Never one to yield to adversity, Cody promptly faced his situation head on. His contract as kiting instructor could be canceled only on six-month notice. With Capper's careful help (Capper dared not come to the attention of the War Office by appearing to directly help Cody and his airplane), Cody negotiated transfer of ownership of the aircraft to himself, so he could continue his experiments. After all, Haldane had said it was worthless!

Capper promptly loaned him the Antoinette engine—all that was available to him. Cody's bravery and good nature had made him a popular figure at Aldershot; the Royal Engineers readily obtained approval for Cody to build a movable shed for his airplane and continue to use the other facilities. With Vivian and Leon helping whenever Capper could spare them from their Army kiting duties, Cody was soon back in business.

Cody flew whenever he could, refining the aircraft. Many friends helped, including off-duty Royal Engineers, a stagehand from *The Klondyke Nugget,* a railway clerk, and even the Codys' gardener!

They shaped struts into streamlined sections and tested them for minimum drag in front of a fan used for inflating hot-air balloons. They modified control surfaces and linkages to provide more feel and balance. Each flight had a purpose, something else to test, something more to learn. Crashes grew less severe, then less frequent, then nearly stopped. Almost daily, the soldiers would see Cody overhead, his turns and climbs and descents becoming close to routine. Spurred on by German threats and fear of aerial warfare, the press started to pay attention again.

But time was running out. Cody would soon have to return the Antoinette engine. The old Antoinette simply had too little power. To turn sharply, Cody had to fly down low and accelerate in the reduced drag of ground effect, then haul the nose up, pirouette around a wingtip, and dive down into ground effect again, completely reversing direction. This trick, which must have appealed to his sense of horsemanship, amazed the growing numbers of spectators, especially those who had seen the skidding, level-wing turns of the French aviators as they hopped about, never climbing more than a few feet off the ground.

Cody wanted enough power to maneuver without aeronautical trickery, no matter how impressive it might look. Using his rapidly shrinking capital from *The Klondyke Nugget*, he ordered a French E.N.V. engine he had originally wanted. Viv and Leon would often return home from their work at the Army Kite School to find their father in his study, the table covered with sketches of the new engine to replace the old Antoinette installation.

The drawings showed a complete rebuild of the airplane. Cody would now sit in front of the new engine, which would be moved to the rear to maintain balance. The controls would be changed, along with a myriad of other details.

When Cody was finally finished with the design, he showed

Cody flies over the Basingstoke Canal.

it to his sons, saying that he had made enough changes that it would no longer be *Army Airplane #1*, but *Cody I*.

Vivian also had exciting news. The Prince and Princess of Wales would be visiting Aldershot to see the Army training maneuvers at Caesar's Camp. The prince had specifically asked to see the kites and the balloons!

Cody's old showman's instincts reemerged. Caesar's Camp was on another part of the garrison, close to his flying field. Why not just happen to fly over at the right time and take a look?

The next day, the Cody family was up before dawn to ready the airplane, so that Viv and Leon would still be able to report later to Capper for kite-flying duties. Carefully timed to coincide with completion of the Army's morning maneuvers before the royal couple, Cody took off and flew over to Caesar's Camp. The troops stopped and waved as he flew overhead. Wheeling around, he flew even lower, leaning over the side of his seat and wildly waving back. To avoid the milling crowds, he landed on top of Danger Hill and slowly taxied back.

The prince was immediately fascinated with Cody's machine. Capper, clearly delighted, was asked to escort the prince and princess over to offer congratulations to Cody. It is not recorded whether Capper was upset when the prince insisted on referring to Cody as "Colonel," which was tantamount to making him a high-ranking officer in the Army. Provided with royal rank or not, Cody graciously accepted their congratulations and put on a royal command performance with a 600-yard flight.

Cody had flown more than a mile. News of this new British record set before royalty spread almost instantly. Cody's supporters in the press watched Cody's every move, and even the naysayers began to recognize his accomplishments. People were becoming more concerned about German threats, the huge new German army, and the threat of bombs from the zeppelins. H. G. Wells speculated on possible aerial warfare. The possibilities of flight were on everyone's mind; Cody quickly became a popular hero.

Lord Northcliffe, the air-minded owner of the *Daily Mirror*, had been dismissed by Secretary of State for War Haldane when he asked why foreign governments were sending representatives to view the Wrights' flights in France, while Britain had sent none. Haldane told him that since experts had said the airplane was useless for warfare, going was unnecessary—and it was highly unlikely that aircraft could cross the oceans to reach England. After all, the Royal Navy and the English Channel had protected England since the days of the Spanish Armada, hundreds of years before.

Lord Northcliffe was annoyed at this imperious brush-off from Haldane. He could see that progress in aviation was coming at a faster and faster pace, so in 1909, he offered a £500 prize (a huge sum at the time) for the first person to fly the Channel. It was won by the Frenchman Louis Blériot in July of the same year.

H. G. Wells promptly noted that militarily, England was no longer an island. For centuries England had felt safe behind the protection of the Royal Navy and the English Channel, but no more. Cody must have watched in delight as the press sung his praises and savaged the shortsightedness of his War Office detractors.

CHAPTER 11

VINDICATION?

Cody made more exceptional flights. Incorporating final changes before swapping the Antoinette for the new E.N.V. engine, Cody made a two-mile circular flight at more than 25 miles per hour, far exceeding his former British record. Then, though he had told reporters he would try no more long flights, he couldn't resist giving the tired but faithful Antoinette a graceful farewell: a four-mile circuit of Laffan's Plain. Another record.

Cody and the boys tore the airplane apart to rebuild it to the new plans. After a couple of weeks of feverish work, the transformed airplane emerged. Among the many changes was a second seat behind the pilot. After a few brief test flights and a minor radiator change, Cody announced that the airplane was ready.

Capper was at the Aldershot encampment when he heard the roar of the E.N.V. engine for the first time. He looked up as Cody rocketed overhead, pulled up into an impossibly steep climbing turn, dived down again, and repeated the same maneuver in the opposite direction, describing a figure eight over the ground.

By now, the Royal Engineers and all the other soldiers were cheering and waving at Cody's show. Capper's heart was in his mouth as he watched

Cody slow and bank to start a steep turn near the ground. When Cody had been in this position before, the airplane had slid into the ground, caught a wingtip, and crashed. This time, Cody jammed the throttle forward. Maintaining the same steep angle, he spiraled upward and headed off to the Balloon Factory shed. Along with what seemed like all the troops in the garrison, Capper set off in hot pursuit.

Capper arrived to find Cody standing on the wing, surrounded by hundreds of Royal Engineers. Leon and Vivian were checking the fuel and oil. Lela and young Frank, along with Mrs. Capper and her daughter, had hitched a ride to the Balloon Factory shed with one of Capper's fellow officers.

Cody looked at Capper and made a theatrical gesture toward the newly installed rear seat. How better to honor his old friend than to take him on England's first airplane passenger flight? He grabbed Capper's hand and swung him up onto the wing and into the passenger's seat. In moments, they were aloft.

They circled the entire encampment. Capper's faith and trust in his friend had again paid off. When they landed, Capper stood on the wing and looked out over the Royal Engineers, many of whom had worked with him and Cody since the first kite flights. Capper led the troops in a rousing "Three Cheers for Cody" and tossed his hat high into the air as hundreds of soldiers roared their approval. Cody would later say that he had never been so moved. Capper then turned to Lela and motioned to the passenger seat. It took little to persuade her. With her skirt secured and her hat tied firmly against the breeze, Lela became the first woman in England to fly. She had always been partner to Cody's dreams and she and the boys had shared them every step of the way. When she fell in love with the American cowboy, could this daughter of Britain ever have envisioned that she would be the first woman to look down on England from the passenger seat of England's first airplane? August 15, 1909, was a remarkable day for the Codys and for British aviation.

Skirts tied down for modesty, Lela awaits her first flight.

Over the next few days each of the boys flew with his father. Dignitaries and friends stood in line to ride with Cody in "the world's first aerial omnibus," as he called it. Cody continued to work on the airplane, improving the radiators in particular.

Soon, it was September 8, 1909, and Cody had one more important goal. Three weeks remained on his Army contract. Cody and his sons pulled the airplane from the shed. The sun was just coming up.

Vivian noted that Cody had on his old high-topped riding boots, which he hadn't worn in years. Cody told the boys that they always brought him luck—and it was cold now that he was sitting out there in front with the new engine.

Cody instructed his sons to rock the wings while he checked the fuel. He needed to get every last air bubble out of the tank, since the flight he now planned would need every drop of fuel. Leon helped Cody warm up the engine while Viv

After a slight landing mishap, Cody uses his old cowboy skills to rope the airplane and pull it back on its wheels.

went and told the official observers they were ready. The flight would go all around the district—Aldershot, then Camberly, then Fleet Farnham, finishing up by coming in from Farnborough—all cross-country, not just circling Laffan's Plain.

Leon pulled the prop through twice, to get fuel in the engine, then Cody switched on the ignition. On the next pull, the engine burst into life. Leon stood on the wing and felt the radiators. Viv returned and handed Leon a small bottle of fuel for a final top-off. He felt the radiators again—up to temperature. He hollered over the rumble of the engine as he jumped down off the wing: "Good luck, Dad!"

The boys watched as Cody roared across Laffan's Plain. The observers' stopwatches clicked as the wheels left the ground. The small knot of people stood in the morning mist as Cody vanished into the hazy distance. It was 6 A.M.

For a while the observers talked of flying adventures, but Viv and Leon started looking at their watches more frequently. As seven o'clock approached, the minute hand might just as well have been the needle on a fuel gauge creeping toward "Empty." Everyone was watching the sky over Farnborough. Finally, when Cody's hour of fuel was almost gone, Leon shouted: "There he is!"

They could hear the engine spitting and coughing as it burned the last of its fuel. But Cody had plenty of altitude and glided over the woods, back to safety.

Sixty-three minutes and more than forty miles cross-country after takeoff, Cody landed back at Laffan's Plain. Stiff with cold, he eased his way to the ground and threw his arms around his sons' shoulders. "Come on, boys, let's go tell Lela I'm back."

The flight smashed the previous cross-country record of twenty-five miles. Cody's flight proved conclusively that it was possible to fly anywhere you wanted, at a speed fast enough to overcome most of the winds. The airplane had arrived in England.

The American cowboy had built England's first airplane and flown it all the way into the world's record books.

FLIGHTS TO FAME

CHAPTER 12

By now the whole world was aviation-mad, and Cody's accomplishments and undisguised passion for flight made him a popular figure. But it was hard for him to push on with all the new ideas he wanted to try. Regardless of Cody's success and public acclaim, and in spite of Capper's help, the War Office was still stringing him out on payments owed on the war kite. Capper advised him to appeal directly to the Treasury Office. The sad truth was that Cody's four years of Army service had left him almost completely broke.

Making the air his theater, Cody looked to early flying demonstrations as a way to make money. He was paid £2,000 to appear at England's first flying meet at Doncaster in October 1909. He flew whenever the terrible English winter weather allowed.

With the funds from Doncaster, he started work on the *Cody II*, a more advanced version of the *Cody I*. During testing, Cody suffered a serious accident when he hit a patch of rough air close to the ground and was thrown out when the airplane crashed nose first. He was knocked unconscious and was bleeding from a bad cut on his head.

Still recovering, Cody flew at an air meet in Bournemouth a few months later. Tragically, this meet saw the death of his young friend C. S. Rolls, when the tail of his modified Wright *Flyer* separated in flight. Cody was among the first to reach the crash, and he felt a profound sense of loss. The aristocratic Rolls had always treated him with the utmost friendship and respect. Rolls, whose car company would continue to flourish under the leadership of his partner, Royce, was the first British airman to die.

Cody at the controls of the *Cody II.*

Sobered, Cody returned to Laffan's Plain and installed two Green & Co. engines in the *Cody II*. They were too heavy; he could not balance their power properly, so he installed a new E.N.V. engine, which transformed the performance enough that he decided to compete for the Michelin Cup, a prestigious trophy and cash prize. It was a contest for the longest flight around a closed course by the end of the year.

His only serious competitors were two young fliers, Alec Ogilvie and Thomas Sopwith. Sopwith would go on to become the founder of the Sopwith Aviation Company, builders of the famed World War I Sopwith *Camel* fighter. Cody opened the contest at Laffan's Plain with a flight of 94½ miles, a new British record.

Sopwith, flying from Brooklands, answered with a flight of 107 miles. Not bad for a young man in his early twenties with just ten hours of flying experience! Cody responded with a flight of 115 miles. Then on December 28, Ogilvie put up a spectacular flight of 140 miles. Foul weather settled in. With only a few days left in 1910, Ogilvie, flying from Camber Sands on the south coast, appeared to have won the prestigious trophy.

But as the writer Graham Wallace said, "Their struggle to remain airborne longest was as exciting as an episode in Cody's *Klondyke Nugget*." None of the men would give up. On December 31, the last day of 1910—a bitterly cold, misty, blustery, thoroughly miserable day—Cody took off from Laffan's Plain, and shortly thereafter Sopwith took off from Brooklands. Unbeknownst to either of them, Ogilvie's final attempt ended in engine failure after only 50 miles.

On and on Cody and Sopwith flew, their supporters on the ground relaying telephone messages back and forth. Finally, numb, faint, and stiff with cold, Sopwith was forced to land after a gallant 150 miles in appalling weather. But Cody kept flying. Eventually, after 4 hours and 47 minutes, he finally ran out of gas and glided back to earth, his beard and mustache encrusted with ice. He had covered 185 1/2 miles, a resounding victory for both pilot and plane. The Michelin Cup was his!

Cody retired the *Cody II* and started work on the *Cody III*, a smaller, lighter, and faster aircraft. His goal was Lord Northcliffe's 1,000-mile "Circuit of Britain" contest, staged to promote flying—and the circulation of his newspaper, the *Daily Mail*. The race attracted well-financed endeavors from the major French manufacturers.

Cody departs on the Circuit of Britain flight.
The spectators are standing on the banking of the famous Brooklands Racetrack.

On July 22, thirty-two entrants showed up at Brooklands for the race, but only twenty-two started. At each stop along the circuit, thousands of spectators thronged to meet the fliers, and the factory entrants were greeted by teams of skilled mechanics. Cody's small band of helpers often worked late into the night to get the airplane ready for the next day's leg of the contest.

The risks taken by these early pioneers to attempt so long a cross-country flight were unbelievable. No one had any knowledge of the perils of weather and difficulties of navigation that they would experience in such an adventure. It took Cody two weeks of nerve-racking flying to complete the course. He was the last of only five finishers, and the first British plane to finish. Well into his forties, Cody had braved rain, mist, fog, turbulence, flying in the dark, crashes, and all-night repairs to complete the course. Nicknamed "Papa Cody" by competitors half his age, Cody was finally gaining the respect he so well deserved.

Cody would use the *Cody III* to win two more Michelin Trophies and set more records. His fame spread far beyond the aviation community. King George V personally congratulated him on winning the trophies when they met at the Olympia Air Show in London. The king continued referring to Cody as "Colonel," as he had when they first met at Caesar's Camp when he was still the Prince of Wales, waiting to ascend the throne. Such warm acceptance by the king, and indeed all of England, warranted a feature article in *Vanity Fair*, the most socially powerful publication of the day. The magazine declared:

> Prophet of flight S. F. Cody has been, conqueror he has lived to be. It is said that his aerial prophecies have been unduly warm. But it is no use being silent under neglect. And it is surely permissible to gossip to newspaper reporters when you know you can make good. None of his prophecies concerning flight have failed. He built the first man-lifting kite, which belongs to the British Army; it is still unpaid for. He built the first British aeroplane that actually flew, to say nothing of its successors . . . and the original record of 40 miles. Since then he has flown to win three Michelin Trophies, and 1,000 miles round England for honor, and the admiration of his adopted countrymen, which is exceeding great. With the dramatic entrances and exits on his great biplanes, he is the British public's chief and best-beloved showman of flight.
>
> —*Vanity Fair*, "Men of the Day," November 1911

Cody had one last obstacle to overcome: Whitehall and the military establishment. Overwhelming pressure from the public, Parliament, and the Crown itself eventually forced the Army into the age of flight. It announced that a contest, the Army Trials, would be held at Larkhill in August of 1912 to select the aircraft to be used for the new Royal Flying Corps. It would be a complete test of every aspect of the machine's performance.

CHAPTER 13

WINNING ON THE WIND

Of course, Cody immediately entered the Army Trials contest at Larkhill. As always, his involvement was not without high drama and complete perseverance. Cody elected to build a large, fast monoplane, or single-winged airplane. (All his previous designs had been biplanes, with two main wings.) Cody's monoplane would not be something like the little scouting aircraft becoming popular in France, but a massive structure, in the same tradition as *Army Airplane #1* and the *Cody I, II,* and *III,* nicknamed the "Flying Cathedrals" by the press because of their size. He started work on *Cody IV* after he purchased a large Austro-Daimler 120-horsepower engine.

He tested the Austro-Daimler by reinstalling it in the *Cody II,* stored at Laffan's Plain. It transformed the old airplane, such that Cody couldn't resist setting yet another flying first, carrying four passengers at once! The engine was a huge success.

Cody now had two airplanes with proven performance records, and the *Cody IV* monoplane promised to be superior to them both, with its streamlined shape, fully enclosed cockpit, and superior engine.

But as happened so many times in Cody's life, adversity reared up. Cody was giving flying lessons

The *Cody II* "Omnibus," re-engined with the Austro-Daimler, carried a record-breaking four passengers, including son Frank at the left rear position.

and rides to support his projects, and the *Cody II* was destroyed in a training crash in April. But Cody was not discouraged, as the new *Cody IV* was proving to be a fast, maneuverable airplane, fulfilling all its designer's expectations.

July 3, 1912, brought total disaster. In the morning, Army Lieutenant H. D. Harvey-Kelly was flying the *Cody III*, while Cody was airborne testing the *Cody IV*. For the first time, Cody saw one of his own airplanes sharing the air with him, as he zoomed past the *Cody III* in his last new creation. But Harvey-Kelly misjudged his landing and caught a wingtip in a tree. He escaped unhurt, but the *Cody III* was severely damaged. Cody was very worried, as he now had no backup aircraft for the Army Trials.

But the worst was yet to happen. While he was testing the *Cody IV*'s ability to make steep turns, the engine suddenly cut out and Cody was forced to land in a farmer's field. The field was clear, but as he landed, a frightened cow ran into the path of the landing plane—with fatal results for both cow and aircraft. The *Cody IV* flipped over on its back in a shattered heap of wood and fabric. Cody escaped unscathed, but only a few weeks before the Larkhill contest, every airplane he could use for competition had been totally wrecked. To make it worse, the local magistrate forced him to pay for the cow, even though eyewitnesses said that the cow had charged the airplane!

The *Cody IV* monoplane was a sleek, fast machine, until it hit a cow.

As always, Cody would not give up—even though just over three weeks remained before the Army Trials. Taking the best pieces from the wrecks, including the undamaged Austro-Daimler engine, he built a new airplane. Cody drove himself relentlessly, aided by his family and friends. In the middle of the frenzied construction, he finally received word that the Treasury Department would pay off all his claims against the Army, a settlement arbitrated by no less a personage than the Chancellor of the Exchequer, Lloyd George, soon to become prime minister. He said, "I do not see why the State should treat a man more shabbily than an ordinary commercial concern would," and awarded Cody £5,000. The money was a valuable boost: not only to resources, but to the morale of Cody and his overworked group of volunteers.

Without time for tests of a radical new aircraft, his design stuck to the best features of the *Cody III*, but from the start, it

Cody tests the strength of the monoplane wing.

was built to carry up to four people. Also, Cody cleverly recognized that with all the many flying tasks he would have to perform, the Army Trials would be just as much a test of pilot as of machine. The *Cody V* was completed in time for a couple of test flights before he flew it to Larkhill on August 2, the very last day to sign in for the Trials.

No one had expected Cody to show up, and no accommodations had been arranged for Cody and his volunteers, some of whom had ridden the sixty-seven miles from Laffan's Plain to Larkhill on bicycles. The Army found accommodations for Cody, but the others were forced to camp out in an aircraft shipping case lent to them by one of the foreign competitors, none of whom had dared risk flying to the contest.

There were literally dozens of tests of each aircraft, including assembly and dismantling, endurance, rate of climb, tests of the engine for idling and its controls, fuel and oil consumption, and takeoff and landing from plowed fields—an area where Cody's rugged "Flying Cathedrals" had a huge edge, from all his experience at Laffan's Plain. The Army would also test the fastest and slowest speeds in the air, and gliding to a landing with the engine shut off, areas where Cody's experience and piloting skills excelled, aided by the powerful Austro-Daimler engine. Each task was judged by an official observer who flew with each pilot.

Just as in the Circuit of Britain race, there were thirty-two entrants. Cody was the only individual to fly his own airplane. All the rest were well-financed teams from the embryonic aviation industry. Names like Breuget, Vickers, Avro, Bristol, and Blériot were on the list, factories that would become major contributors to worldwide aviation. Their entries were flown by skilled paid pilots like Tom Sopwith and tended by teams of supporting engineers and mechanics.

Cody and his handful of volunteers were alone. His official observer, Lieutenant C. Bettington, sat beside him, noting Cody's performance with slide rule and stopwatch. The trials would last for an arduous thirty days and force planes and pilots to take to the air in all kinds of wind and weather. One by one, contestants failed to pass a test, broke down, or crashed. Mersey Aviation's monoplane crashed, killing its pilot. Cody flew on, rarely winning a test outright, but passing them all.

At the end of the trials, on August 30, 1912, the *Cody V* was one of only four aircraft to complete all the tests. No other British entrant had finished. Cody's skill as a pilot—and his astute recognition that consistency and all-around performance and reliability would win the contest—gave him a cumulative score that topped the entire list of entries. Cody won both the national and international prizes, a grand total of £5,000 and an order for a duplicate of the winning aircraft. The London *Times* wrote of his victory: "This grey-bearded old man has defeated the best the world could bring into competition with him. . . . There will be few in the country who will not be proud of the old man's achievement, since he had done it all himself."

Cody and his *Cody V*, assembled from bits and pieces and wrecks of his earlier aircraft, just weeks before the first Military Trials. He won.

Congratulations poured in from every quarter. General Sir Douglas Haig and his staff arrived to convey King George's personal message of congratulations and to arrange a royal demonstration of the *Cody V* at Hardwick Camp near Cambridge. Cody was delighted to comply.

He was given public parades before thousands of well-wishers in Farnborough and Aldershot, and a standing ovation when he and Lela were introduced at a musical performance

A success at last.

at the Theatre Royal. The Royal Aero Club awarded him its highest honor. But more important to Cody was a letter bearing the heartfelt congratulations of his old friend Colonel Capper. In a certain sad paradox for Capper, his success with aviation had led to his promotion in the Army ranks, so he was no longer involved in aviation. He went on to distinguished service as a general in France during World War I.

Cody was on top of the world. But he could not surrender his passion for flight. Unlike Sopwith and many other pioneers who gave up the skies to establish major aircraft companies, Cody just had to fly. He had his eyes on two prizes, each of which would require a new design. Lord Northcliffe would stage a "Coastal Circuit of Britain" floatplane race with a prize of £5,000. His paper, the *Daily Mirror,* would also set a standing prize of £10,000 for the first flight across the Atlantic. For the transatlantic flight, Cody sketched the *Cody VII*, a huge monoplane aircraft for a crew of three, including a layout for a 400-horsepower twelve-cylinder engine that he intended to have built.

But the Coastal Circuit came first, and the *Cody VI* soon appeared. It was tested on floats in the Basingstoke Canal to make sure it rested on the water at the right angle, then was fitted with wheels for the initial flight tests. A development of the "Cathedral" series of biplanes, the wingspan was 60 feet.

Flight tests went well, and Cody felt sure of winning Lord Northcliffe's latest contests. But it was not to be. On August 7, 1913, while giving a ride to the famous cricket player W.H.B. Evans, the *Cody VI* broke up in midair. Cody and Evans fell to earth and were killed instantly. The *Cody VII*, yet unbuilt, would never fly back to America.

FARNBOROUGH AND THE TREE

CHAPTER 14

Today the fields at Laffan's Plain and Farnborough Common, where Cody performed so many of his tests, are a crisscross of huge runways, hangars, research buildings, and test facilities belonging to the Royal Aircraft Establishment (R.A.E.), now D.E.R.A., the British Defence Establishment Research Agency.

A major event of the aeronautical year, as it has been for almost a century, is the Farnborough Air Show. At every show, the place where Cody first flew echoes to the roar of jets of the latest in modern aircraft technology. When the world's fastest aircraft, the Lockheed *YF-12*, designed by Kelly Johnson and built in his famous Skunk Works, set its longest record in 1965, it flew from California to Farnborough. Farnborough and the Royal Aircraft Establishment have witnessed and participated in virtually every aeronautical advance since Cody's first flight there in 1908.

The echoes of jets also wash over a strange aluminum tree. For years, it was a real tree, the one to which Cody had tied his airplane to try out his ingenious adjustable-pitch propellers and test their thrust. After Cody's death, Farnborough's pilots, researchers, and workers kept the original tree alive.

Cody's Tree. The replica built by the Royal Aircraft Factory.

When it could no longer be preserved, they erected The Tree—a metal reproduction of the original, made of aluminum, the light, strong metal used for so much of aircraft construction. There is a plaque mounted on it, to perpetuate the memory of Cody's contributions.

Controversy, which had marked so many events in Cody's life, shrouded his fatal accident as well. Cody had used single bracing wires in critical places and took a fatalistic attitude toward what might happen if one broke. Only a few weeks before his fatal crash, Cody had told Harry Harper, aviation reporter for the *Daily Mail*, that if he were to die, he hoped it might be "swift and sudden, death from one of my own aeroplanes." Still dreaming of the future, Cody got his wish.

The whole nation mourned his loss. The king sent the commander of the Army, General Sir Douglas Haig, to convey his personal condolences to Lela. He reflected on seeing Cody at Aldershot on several occasions and paid tribute to his "dogged determination and dauntless courage." The Army paid Cody the unprecedented homage of burying him with full honors at the military cemetery on the hilltop overlooking Aldershot. Representatives of every British regiment marched in his funeral procession.

Many had seen him with his war kites on maneuvers and later flying above Laffan's Plain. They all wanted to honor the bravery of the flamboyant yet likable cowboy who had led aviation from balloons and kites to the birth of the Royal Flying Corps. So many people sent wreaths that the Royal Flying Corps had to provide several trucks to carry them. Lela's floral aircraft control wheel lay alone atop the coffin as the Army cortege escorted the horse-drawn gun carriage that carried it past the 50,000 mourners who lined the route of the procession.

Lela went into seclusion after Cody's death. When she died in 1939, she was buried next to him in the Aldershot military cemetery.

After Cody's death, his sons stayed in aviation. Vivian worked with the Royal Aircraft Establishment as head of the Fabric Shop. His work, especially on parachutes, gained him the British Empire Medal. After forty years, he retired. When he died in 1961, he was buried next to his parents at Aldershot. Leon made a brief return to the stage, yet returned to work with the British Navy on kites and balloons. He eventually went to work for the Handley Page aircraft factory, until he died in the early 1940s.

Frank was the only one who felt the tug of adventure that had taken Cody up into the sky. Like Cody, he became a pilot, joining the Royal Flying Corps that his father had done so much to create. He was killed in air combat with four German fighters in France during World War I, while flying with No. 41 Squadron of the Royal Flying Corps.

Over 50,000 people, including representatives from the Royal Navy and every regiment in the British Army, attended Cody's funeral procession.

In many ways, Cody's life paralleled the Wrights', even though they approached the problems of flight from entirely different directions. Where the Wrights were logical, Cody was intuitive. Yet of all the early pioneers, these three spent the most time in the air before their successful powered flights: Cody with his kites and hang glider, the Wrights with their gliding tests at Kitty Hawk. They were all brave, clever men, avid experimenters, and keen observers. Like Cody, Wilbur Wright died at the height of his fame, at forty-five, albeit from typhoid rather than a flying accident.

Until 1948, Cody's airplane and the original Wright *Flyer* "flew" side by side, suspended from the ceiling of the Science Museum in London. Because of disputes over the Smithsonian Institution's recognition of who was first to fly, Orville Wright had given the machine to the British, for exhibition in the Kensington Science Museum in London. There it stayed until after Orville's death, when the Smithsonian finally and unequivocally recognized the Wrights as the first to fly. The Wright *Flyer* was returned to America.

What remains of Samuel Franklin Cody's legacy? Cody, more than anyone else, showed the possibilities of flight to the British people—it was not just a sport for the aristocracy, or a tool for the military. His enthusiasm and showmanship did much to create the atmosphere that nurtured the English pioneers of early aviation like Sopwith, who put the country in the forefront of flying during the dark days of the great World Wars. His technical contributions were overshadowed by the Wrights' accomplishment. But Cody achieved all his goals on his own, with only the help of his family and the support of Colonel Capper. This, perhaps more than anything else, accounted for the affection in which the public held him. He made the adventure of flight personal and possible for the common man.

A LIFE FULL OF AIRPLANES

APPENDIX A

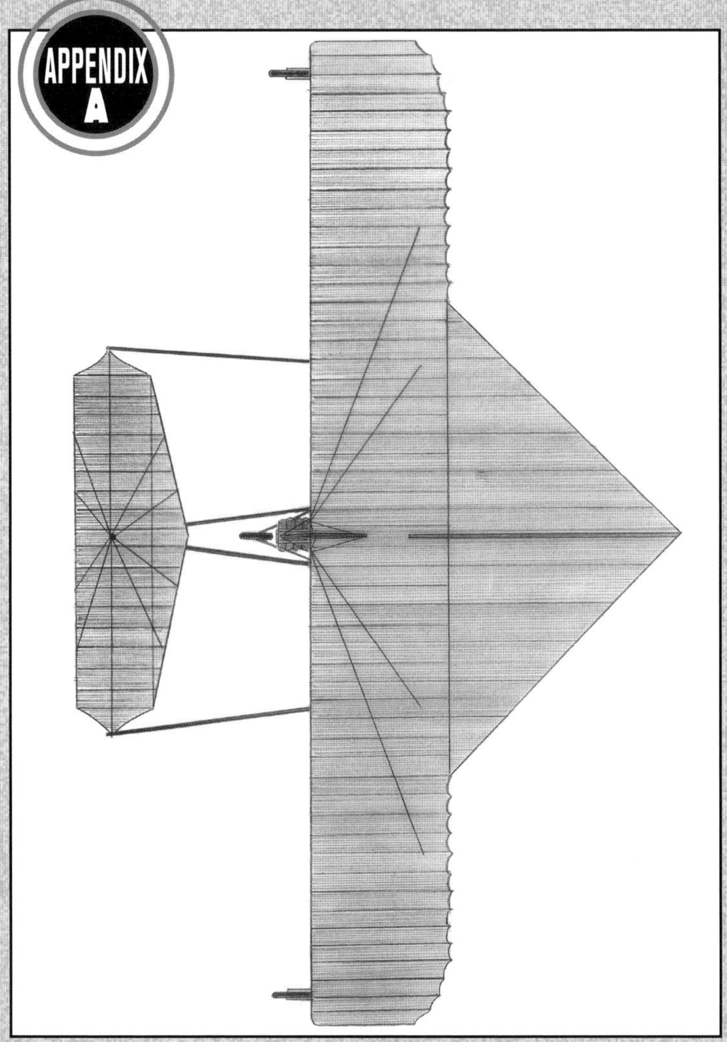

The story of Cody's life can be told by his airplanes. He made them all fly very well, but sometimes only after many adventures and hardships.

Army Airplane #1, 1908. Cody's (and England's) first powered aircraft, in which he made his first flights. It went through many changes with each crash and rebuild. It became the *Cody I* when he was discharged from his employment at the Balloon Factory. It had a span of 52 feet, a length of 32 feet, a wing area of 790 square feet, and a speed of 38 to 40 miles per hour.

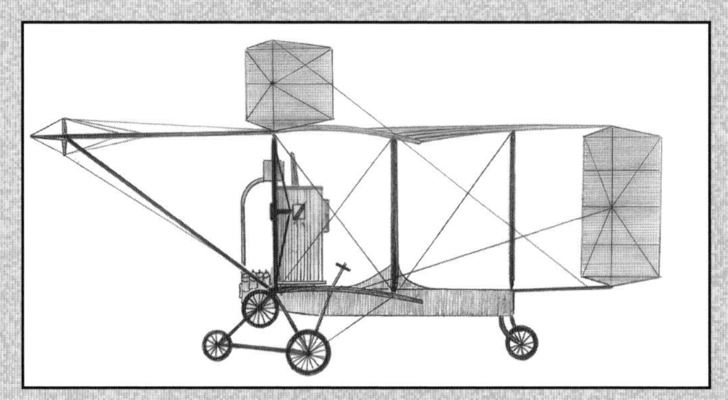

Cody's *Army Airplane #1.*

Cody II, 1910. After his success in meeting all the terms of the Army contract, even after he was fired, Cody went on to many other triumphs. The *Cody II* started out with a twin-engine design and was later converted to an 80-horsepower E.N.V. engine. It performed well enough to win the prestigious Michelin Trophy for the greatest distance covered, then it was put in storage. It was later re-engined with a 120-horsepower Austro-Daimler, thereby enabling it to carry four people: the pilot and three passengers.

The *Cody II* had a span of 46 feet, was 34 feet in length, and had a wing area of 540 square feet. In its final form, it weighed more than a ton, flew at 65 miles per hour, and had a range of 200 miles.

Cody III, 1911. Cody built this airplane for the 1911 Circuit of Britain race, sponsored by the *Daily Mail*. Although it placed only fifth in the contest, Cody used it to win two more Michelin Trophies, for both endurance and distance, in September and October 1911. It was the smallest of Cody's airplanes, and used wing warping instead of ailerons.

The *Cody III* had a span of 40 feet and length of 130 feet. It weighed 1,750 pounds empty, and had a speed of 58 miles per hour and a range of 350 miles.

Cody IV, 1912. This was Cody's only monoplane aircraft, a side-by-side two-seater powered by his 120-horsepower Austro-Daimler engine. It was built for the Military Trials, to be held at Larkhill in 1912, but the engine cut off in flight. In the ensuing emergency landing, Cody hit a cow, destroying the airplane and killing the cow, for which Cody later had to reimburse the farmer.

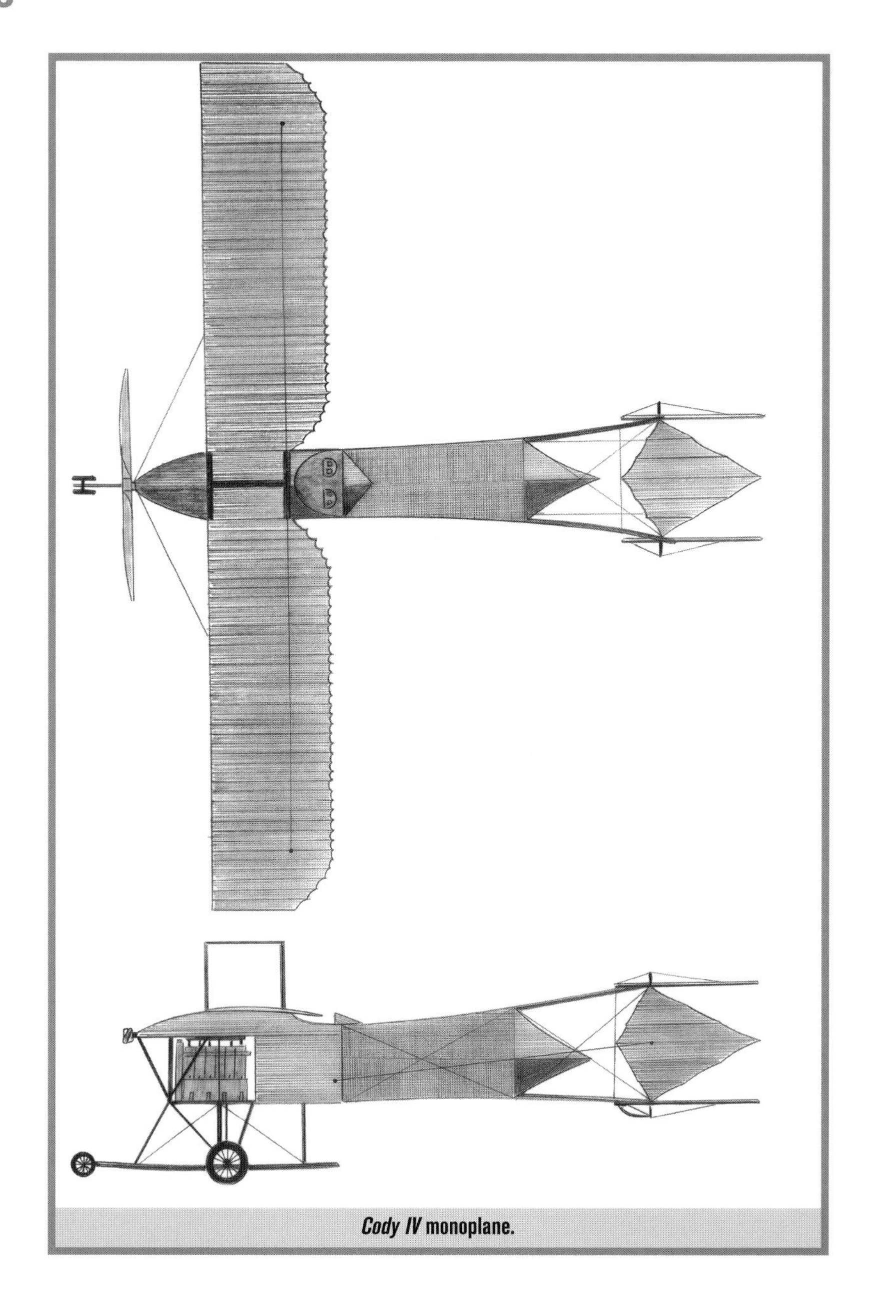

***Cody IV* monoplane.**

The aircraft had a span of 43 feet 6 inches, a length of 37 feet 6 inches, a wing area of 260 square feet, and a weight of 2,400 pounds. It was considered quite fast, with a top speed of 83 miles per hour.

Cody V, 1912. Cody and his friends assembled this airplane from bits of *Cody III* and *IV*. Working night and day, Cody and his band of helpers finished the airplane in less than a month. It won the Military Trials, thanks perhaps more to Cody's airmanship than to the innate excellence of the design. Cody borrowed the airplane back from the Army and used it to enter—and win—the 1912 Michelin Trophy contest. A second airplane was ordered as part of the prize for winning the Trials, and this airplane survives in the Kensington Science Museum in London, the only remaining Cody aircraft.

The *Cody V* had a span of 43 feet, a length of 37 feet 9 inches, a wing area of 485 square feet, and an empty weight of 1,948 pounds, with a top speed of 72 miles per hour.

Cody VI, 1913. Cody's last airplane. It was built for the 1913 Circuit of Britain race, a floatplane contest. Cody tested the floats on the Basingstoke Canal, then fitted wheels for the initial flight testing. The flight performance of the airplane exceeded Cody's expectations. But on August 7, Cody and his passenger were killed when the structure failed in midair.

It was a large airplane, with a span of 59 feet 6 inches, a length of 40 feet 9 inches, a wing area of 770 square feet, and a top speed of 70 miles per hour.

Cody VII, designed 1913. At the time of his death, Cody had

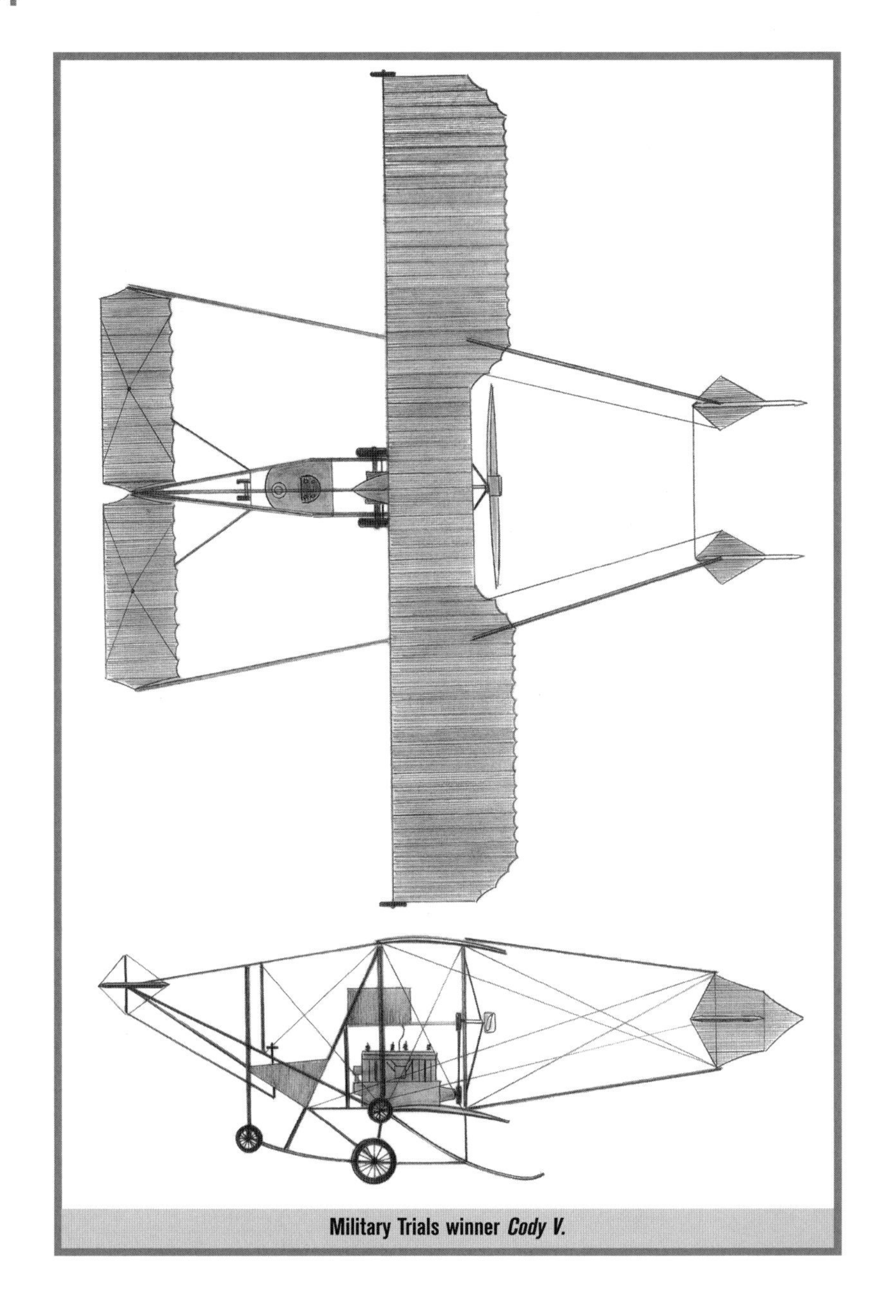

Military Trials winner ***Cody V.***

completed the preliminary design of a 100-foot-wingspan plane to fly back to the United States, his birthplace. He had ordered a 400-horsepower engine to power the huge craft. He had hoped to capture the £10,000 prize offered by Lord Northcliffe and the *Daily Mail* for the first flight across the Atlantic, a prize won seven years later by Captain John Alcock and Lieutenant Arthur Whitten Brown, flying a Vickers *Vimy* (Charles Lindbergh, the American aviator, later made the first solo transatlantic crossing in 1927). Would Samuel Cody have made it? Was he attempting too big a leap? He had made every one of his previous designs work—and work well.

For aviation historians, there is a wealth of records, photographs, and relics that can be found if you look hard enough. You can still go to Farnborough and see Cody's Tree. It is just in front of the Cody Building. And Cody's Army Trials airplane, the *Cody V*, still hangs suspended, flying across the ceiling of the Kensington Science Museum in London, near where the original Wright brothers' aircraft once hung. You can go there and see it yourself.

1900 Count von Zeppelin flies the first of his slender, rigid airships.

Orville and Wilbur Wright arrive at North Carolina with camping gear, food, glider, mandolin, and the first camera seen in Kitty Hawk.

1901 Cody applies for kite patent.

Cody demonstrates kites to Major Trollope of the British Army.

Wrights leave Kitty Hawk very discouraged. Wilbur tells Orville he thinks it will be a thousand years before flying is possible.

1902 Lela goes aloft in Cody's kite, probably the first woman to fly in a heavier-than-air machine.

The Wrights invent the modern aircraft control system, which provides three-axis control of wingtips and nose in all dimensions. They have just unlocked the secrets of flight. Orville and Wilbur write to their family, "All doubts resolved . . . success assured."

1903 Cody flies kite from Royal Navy vessel.

Orville Wright makes the first true powered flight at Kitty Hawk—taking off, climbing, maintaining altitude, and landing all under his control.

1905 Cody becomes Army kiting instructor, and builds glider kite.

Einstein publishes paper claiming $E=mc^2$ (energy equals mass times the speed of light squared).

1907 Cody and Colonel Capper fly the airship *Nulli Secundus* to London.

1908 Wrights make their first truly public flight in France.

Cody makes the first airplane flight in England.

Henry Ford sells the first Model T automobile.

1909 Lela and Colonel Capper fly with Cody, the first passengers in England. Cody makes a world-record cross-country flight.

1910 Cody wins Michelin Trophy.

1911 Cody places fifth in the Circuit of Britain contest. He also wins two more Michelin Trophies.

1912 Cody wins Military Trials and one more Michelin Trophy.

1913 Cody is killed in a crash of the *Cody VI*.

Nowadays, we take air travel almost for granted, not thinking about the technical marvels that allow over 800,000 pounds of Boeing 747 to climb over eight miles up into the sky and span nearly half the globe nonstop. The modern passenger is much more likely to worry about making a connection at the giant airports, where all the flights seem to try to arrive and take off at the same time. Thus, "delayed in Dallas."

But if you sit in the seat that looks out of the front and address the runway with intent to fly, all the magic is still there.

AUTHOR'S NOTE, ACKNOWLEDGMENTS, AND SELECTED SOURCES

The process of writing *Rider in the Sky* turned out to be very different from what I expected. With a lifetime interest in flying, I thought the research would be quite straightforward. Then I ran into Cody's early life. A judicious review of previously accepted dates and photographs soon shows that the ages and dates of his early life just don't fit. Cody's early years are still pretty much a mystery, especially the development of his talent as an engineer and designer. This led me to the Internet.

A pattern soon emerged such that if I dived down the Alice-in-Wonderland hole of a Google search (with Cody keywords, of course), I would find myself meeting wonderful people in fascinating places. I cannot say enough about Jean Roberts, an amateur historian who actually lives in Cody's house. Her work in cataloging events in Cody's life and locating so much of his memorabilia in museums all over the world has improved scholarship on his life in a way that puts many of the earlier aviation historians to shame. And she continues to work away at further understanding Cody's impact. She also runs the wonderful Cody Web site at www.sfcody.org.uk.

One of the places the Internet led me was to the Drachen Foundation in Seattle, Washington. (*Drachen* is German for "kite," as well as "dragon.") They have a huge collection of kiting materials that spans ancient history to the present day, as well as a magnificent Cody archive. Many thanks to Ali Fujino and Lesley Noonan and their work in getting me so many marvelous images for this book. Their Web site is at www.drachen.org. Every teacher should go there and click on the "education" button.

Digging into Cody's cowboy past led me to the Autry Museum of Western Heritage in Los Angeles. They were tremendously helpful, but I got sidetracked by some of their incredible programs. If you visit their Web site at www.autry-museum.org, be sure to go to the store section and look at the marvelous poster for the museum's *Women of the Wild West* presentation. The Autry Museum is an absolutely wonderful education resource for both Internet and real-time visits.

In England, the National Science Museum, the British Museum, the Museum of Army Flying, and the Imperial War Museum all made valuable contributions to the book, beginning with the Web. For me, the Internet worked as a communications medium to link me to people and museums and libraries. Coupled with e-mail and cheap long-distance phone calls, it allowed me access to primary sources in a way that simply would not have been possible only a few years ago. This added greatly to the richness of Cody's history.

As far as the literature, anyone interested in aviation beyond the superficial retracings of well-known figures should look at the journal *WWI Aero* and its companion publication, *Skyways* magazine. Leo Opdyke and his band of volunteers have done an incredible job of saving irreplaceable records from aviation history, including much about Cody. And where else could you find such little gems as the *Friesly Falcon*, the first airplane to fly an entire baseball team to a game and later disappear to China? Their Web site is www.ww1aeroplanesinc.org.

Except for two publications, much of the literature on Cody is scattered throughout specialized aviation history. The two books are *The Flying Cathedral* by Arthur Stanley Lee Gould, published by Methuen & Co. in 1965, which is based on the family's version of Cody's past but really captures Cody's intelligence and irrepressible character; and the more recent *Colonel Cody and the Flying Cathedral* by Garry Jenkins, published by Simon & Schuster in 1999, which is far more historically correct. It is interesting to compare the books to see how different two interpretations of history can be.

For the young reader to learn about just what it took to be an early pilot, as well as to realize the richness of primary resources, there is no better author than Orville Wright himself in his short and easy book *How We Invented the Airplane*, edited by Fred C. Kelly, first published in 1953 by David McKay Company and republished in 1988 by Dover Press. Orville wrote the material, which included less than twenty pages of text, in 1920.

Far and away the best book for access to the history and literature of early aviation is Tom Crouch's book *The Bishop's Boys*, published by W.W. Norton & Company in 1990. This marvelously readable yet very scholarly work not only tells the entire history of the Wrights but gives the reader all the sources needed to find the true history of aviation's pioneers.

As Lilienthal said, "To fly is everything," and I wanted to capture some of the excitement that Cody and Capper certainly felt. Over the years, a whole flying vernacular has grown up. Marvelous expressions like "shooting the breeze" and "hangar flying" have been created to describe pilots' conversations. While all the dialogue between Cody and Capper is a figment of my imagination, I'm sure that the matters they discuss in the book are the very things that they would have talked about as they took those first brave steps into the air.

And last but by no means least, I needed an editor to take me from being a pilot and scientist to being enough of a writer to tell Cody's marvelous story. Michelle Frey could not have been more patient and helpful.

INDEX